BEN STOKES

Studies in Religion
*Series editor: W. N. Greenwood*

# Facing the issu

*Barbara Wintersgill*

Nelson

Thomas Nelson and Sons Ltd
Nelson House   Mayfield Road
Walton-on-Thames   Surrey
KT12 5PL   UK

51 York Place
Edinburgh
EH1 3JD   UK

Thomas Nelson (Hong Kong) Ltd
Toppan Building 10/F
22A Westlands Road
Quarry Bay   Hong Kong

Thomas Nelson Australia
102 Dodds Street
South Melbourne
Victoria 3205   Australia

Nelson Canada
1120 Birchmount Road
Scarborough Ontario
M1K 5G4   Canada

© Barbara Wintersgill 1987

First published by Macmillan Education Ltd 1987
(under ISBN 0-333-38299-4)

This edition published by Thomas Nelson and Sons Ltd 1991

ISBN 0-17-437102-0
NPN 9 8 7 6 5 4 3

Printed in Hong Kong.

# Contents

# Acknowledgements

The author and publishers wish to acknowledge the following photograph sources:

Andes Press Agency, p. 47
Barnaby's Picture Library, pp. 33, 55
BBC Hulton Picture Library, p. 116
Board of Deputies of British Jews, p. 75
British Kidney Patient Association, p. 105
British Tourist Authority, p. 24
Jim Brownbill, pp. 29(B), 36, 38, 114
Camera Press, pp. 18, 20(T), 28(B), 82, 119
Catholic Pictorial, Liverpool , p. 20(B)
Ron Chapman, p. 55
Christian Aid, p. 32
Stephanie Colasanti, p. 70
Commonwealth Institute, p. 55
Corrymeela Link, p. 124
Chris Fairclough, p. 30(B)
GEC Industrial Controls Ltd, p. 37(T)
Sally and Richard Greenhill, p. 37(B)
Lucas Aerospace Ltd, p. 106
Medical Research Council, p. 103
Photo Source, pp. 13, 14, 48, 53, 93
Popperfoto, pp. 52, 86, 120, 121(T), 127, 135
Roger Rawlinson, pp. 123
David Richardson, pp. 67, 71
Save the Children Fund, pp. 27(L), 29(T), 30(T)
Science Photo Library, p. 96(T)
Spastics Society, p. 110(T)
Sunday Times/British Friends of Neve Shalom, p. 125
Liba Taylor, pp. 17, 55
Topham Picture Library, pp. 73, 121(B)
UNICEF, p. 25
World Bank Photo by Yosef Hader, p. 28(T)
Viewpoint, pp. 96(B), 110(B)

Cover by kind permission of the Trustees of the Tate Gallery.

The publishers have made every effort to trace the copyright holders, but where they have failed to do so they will be pleased to make the necessary arrangements at the first opportunity.

# Preface

Religious Education has undergone profound changes in the recent past. This series, *Studies in Religion,* has been planned to take account of these changes with reference to both syllabus content and to those skills of learning which are now required of the student. While each book is independent of others in the series, the general approach adopted by the authors is similar. Each writer has in mind the student who is preparing for entry to public examinations in Religious Studies at 16+ and provision is made for students of a wide range of ability.

Each book, therefore, contains basic factual information together with 'extension material' which gives scope for work at a deeper level and/or further factual material for those who work more quickly. The text also incorporates 'stimulus material' to promote discussion and to foster the skills of understanding and evaluation; these skills are then applied by the student to written work in response to questions.

The approach which is characteristic of this series is one which is objective, fair and balanced. The reader is encouraged to consider a number of differing approaches to the subject matter and to respond to 'the challenging and varied nature of religion' (cf. Aim 2 of the National Criteria for Religious Studies, 1985). The first books to be published will bring new perspectives to bear on 'traditional' areas (the Synoptic Gospels and Social and Moral Issues) and to an area which features prominently in all recent syllabuses for 16+ examinations: 'Christianity'.

W.N. Greenwood
*Series editor*

# Note to students

If you are reading this book, you are probably studying a course with a name like 'Contemporary Religious and Social Issues'. You may be studying for an examination or you may be taking this course as part of your core studies. In any event, I hope that you will find this book an interesting challenge.

Do not be put off by the fact that the book is concentrating on religious responses to matters arising in everyday life. It is possible that only a few people in your group hold a religious belief, and you should find that this book makes no assumptions about your faith (although it does assume that you have studied RE for at least three years) nor does it expect you to agree with any particular point of view. This book asks you to do three things in particular:

(a) Think for yourself about the issues raised.

(b) Understand why certain customs and attitudes have become accepted in society.

(c) Realise that where a religious viewpoint is given, whether or not you agree with it, it is an opinion held by many people, and you should be tolerant of it. In the course of your study you will need to discuss certain topics with other people. If you disagree with someone's point of view, try to say *why* you disagree, and try not to use words like 'stupid' of other people's opinions, for that will simply give offence.

By the time you have finished working with this book, you will have realised that a great many views are held on all matters, even by people who follow the same religion. You probably know that there are a number of Christian groups, called 'denominations', most of which issue statements about their beliefs. This is equally the case with other religions which also have their divisions. It is not possible to cover every group's view on every subject in this book or we would run into several volumes! However, you will find that with each topic some of the most influential religious views are discussed. But even then – be careful! It would be wrong even to suppose that all Roman Catholics believe the same thing on any issue, or that all Methodists agree on all points.

Religious Education is a frustrating subject to some people because it does not give any right answers – or perhaps it would be more true to say that it offers many right answers. This book does not give any right answers except to purely factual questions. You may have heard older people say that the more you know, the more you realise what you do not know. This is certainly the case with religion. Many people say that they have arrived at a religious conviction through experience. If this is the case we should never regard our opinions as 'finally formed', or our studies complete, since life is always presenting us with new situations which may confirm or change our previous understanding.

There is a true story which illustrates very well the problems which a book like this one may raise. In 1983 there was a parliamentary debate about bringing back capital punishment. During a class discussion on the subject in one school, a pupil suggested that there should be a referendum on such an important matter. One girl said immediately, 'Well, I know how I'd vote: I'd hang the lot of them' (referring to murderers). 'But', said someone else, 'don't you think that if your vote meant life or death to several people, you should at least sit down and think about it for a while before making up your mind?' The girl probably spoke for many of us when she replied: 'If you spent your whole life thinking about what you ought to do you'd never get anything done.'

You might begin by asking if anyone in your group has been in a situation calling for action where the arguments over what was the *right* thing to do have been so complicated that they have simply acted on instinct. You might also ask them if, in retrospect, they think they did the right thing!

# Note to teachers

'Something to discuss and write about'.... As pupils work through each chapter they will find sections entitled 'Something to discuss and write about' at regular intervals. The suggestions for discussion and written work (which are by no means exhaustive) take basically the same form every time. The author has deliberately avoided suggesting varied activities such as 'Organise a debate on ...' or 'Prepare a group presentation of ...' or 'Write and perform a drama to explain the view that ...' There are reasons for avoiding setting out this sort of activity in a textbook:

(a) RE is notoriously a subject to which anything from one to four periods a week may be allotted. Teachers have vastly differing periods of time in which to complete a course, and it would not be fair to those with little time to confront their pupils with exciting but time-consuming activities which would preclude their completing the syllabus.

(b) RE groups vary considerably in their composition. Some contain as few as five pupils, others over thirty. Some are of mixed ability, while others are setted. An activity which may be suitable for one group may not be appropriate for another.

(c) Teachers have their individual styles. In teaching material of this kind, some prefer to work with small groups, others would rather class-teach.

For these reasons the author has suggested topics which should be considered, but leaves it to the individual teacher to decide how best to put those ideas to good use within the context of the group being taught.


## Some practical hints

1 Some of the facts and figures in this book will inevitably become out of date. It is therefore necessary to encourage pupils to watch current affairs programmes and read a newspaper. Always try to relate the principles you are discussing to real-life issues.

2 'Soap operas' can be of great value. When discussing say illegitimacy or homosexuality, pupils are often tempted to hold up one of their aquaintance as an example. This is not to be encouraged, and the use of fictional characters in programmes like *Coronation Street* or *East-Enders* provides a 'real-life' example while keeping the personal element out of discussion.

3 Always publicise the content of your syllabus to other departments. The chapters in this book do not have to be tackled in any
particular order, and you may find for example that you are able to
begin a unit on world poverty alongside the Geography department's
work on the same subject.

# 1 Making decisions

There are some people who believe that subjects such as those dealt with in this book should not form part of a Religious Education course at all. They would say that an RE course should concentrate on the phenomena of religion such as festivals and worship, or on belief in God or life after death. They might argue that thinking about problems such as abortion or the Third World is not restricted to religious people, and would argue that such subjects belong in a Moral Education or Social Studies course. However, although it is quite true to say that everyone thinks about these matters, be they Christian, Muslim or Marxist, the answers which they give to questions about everyday life might well depend on their individual philosophy of life or their religion. True, not everyone has a personal philosophy or religion, but in this book we will be looking at some of the judgements made by people who do have a belief, and we will be seeing just how that belief affects their judgement. We will also be considering to what extent traditional religious ideas have influenced the thinking of non-religious people.

> **Something to discuss and write about**
> Try this simple exercise which looks at how people behave in relation to what they believe. Copy this chart into your workbook and list the 'beliefs' in column A. Then in column B write down how a person holding this belief might behave. The first one has been done for you.

| A | B |
|---|---|
| 1 Ann believes that it is wrong to kill animals for their fur. | 1 Ann takes part in protest marches against a local mink farm. |
| 2 Paul believes that it is wrong to kill animals for their meat. | |
| 3 The Jones family are Christians who believe that all good things, such as their food, come from God, and that they should give him thanks for it. | |
| 4 Abdul is a strict Muslim. He believes that his parents will find him a suitable wife when the time comes. | |
| 5 Mr and Mrs Cohen believe very strongly that their children should be brought up as Orthodox Jews. They want the children to mix with gentiles as little as possible. | |

Many religious groups give their members guidance as to how they should behave by laying down certain rules and laws. These laws are often to be found in the sacred texts of the religion. Of course, not everyone who is religious will follow these rules unquestioningly, but many believers do feel that the basic rules of their religion should be followed as far as possible. For example, there are many Christians and Jews who take the command to 'keep the Sabbath day holy' very seriously. They will not take on any job which requires them to work on a Sunday or Saturday respectively.

---

### Group work

1 Can you name two religions *apart from* Christianity which contain in their teaching a set of rules or laws? Can you name any of these laws?
2 Look up the following passages in the New Testament. What do they suggest about the connection between believing that Jesus taught the right way to live and the way you behave?

  (a) John 13:4–5, 12–15.
  (b) Matthew 5:38–42, 43–44.
  (c) Matthew 6:14–15.
  (d) Matthew 6:24.
  (e) Matthew 25:31–46.

---

### The reason for an action – does it matter?

Some people say that there are times when it is very important to know why a person has behaved in a certain way. Take the case of two very old ladies, both bedridden, both in considerable pain, and both nearing the ends of their lives. Each old lady was cared for by a niece. Eventually one of the these young women killed her aunt by injecting air into her veins, thus causing heart failure. The other killed her aunt by suffocating her. In the course of the two murder trials that followed, it became clear that whereas one killing was carried out with the intention of sparing the old lady further pain, in the other case the main motive was the legacy of $10 000 left to the niece.

*What do you think?*

Do you think that the court should have taken the motives of these two young women into account when deciding on a verdict and in passing sentence?

Try to think of other examples of the same action being performed by different people for different motives.

Try to go further and think of identical actions which are carried out in different circumstances, where you think that one circumstance could have made the action right and the other made it wrong.

## The Gnostic answer

Read this section carefully. It may help to throw an interesting light on some of the attitudes you will find later on in the book.

From about the second century BC to the second century AD there existed throughout southern Europe and the Near East a number of religious groups whom we link under the name Gnostics. Their attitude to moral behaviour is worth looking at because we still find it in some forms today. Gnosticism was a religion which contained many Christian ideas in its teaching, but unlike Christians Gnostics were *metaphysical dualists*. This means that they regarded all material things, including the body, as being the evil creations of a lesser, even evil, god; whilst the soul and all spiritual (non-material) things were seen as being good, and the creation of the supreme god. Many Gnostics believed that once your soul was saved, nothing your body did could change your destiny. Once your soul was liberated, your body could do what it liked as though it had nothing to do with your true self at all. As a result, many Gnostics had a reputation for immoral behaviour. It must also be pointed out, however, that a few Gnostic groups took a totally opposite point of view. They also believed that the body was evil, but instead of saying that their bodies were not their responsibility, they worked to overcome the desires of the flesh and lived lives of extreme self-denial. (Try to think of any Christian groups who might have been influenced by this way of thinking.) The important thing to remember is that the Gnostics believed that the body and soul were two separate things: they did not together form the whole personality.

## Are the answers in the Scriptures?

Every religion has its sacred texts, and these texts often provide guidelines as to how people should behave as well as what they should believe. Many of the rules set by religions are not easy to follow because they are very demanding and often require considerable sacrifices. Let us take the New Testament as an example of how people who belong to a religion, in this case Christianity, regard their Sacred Scriptures.

For those who say that to be a Christian you should live as Jesus lived and follow his commands, there is plenty of evidence in the Gospels. You have already looked at some of these passages, but consider these also and say what guidance they give.

1 Matthew 5:22.
2 Matthew 5:28.
3 Matthew 5:32.
4 Matthew 5:44.

Do you think that some of these rules are more difficult for people to follow today than they were at the time of Jesus? Do you think that to be a Christian you *must* live by these guidelines?

The teaching of Jesus occupies a fraction of the space in the Bible as a whole. We have already seen that some Christians may try to model their lives on that of Jesus, and you have probably met Christians, or Jews, who give as their reason for a certain belief or action, 'Well, the Bible says so', as though no further explanation was needed. But this is not the attitude towards the Bible held by all Christians.

---

**Something to discuss**

Here are five Christians talking about the Bible. Which view, if any, do you most agree with, and which do you think represents the most popular Christian point of view?

---

(a) 'The Bible is the world of God dictated to his prophets and people with extraordinary insight and understanding. Every word of it is true and it contains everything a person needs to believe in order to be saved. Every commandment in the Bible must be followed absolutely.' (People who take this point of view may refer you to passages like these:
Isaiah 2:1; Amos 9:1; John 6:63, 68; 2 Timothy 3:16.)

(b) 'The Bible provides a basis for Christian belief, but it has to be interpreted. The Church leaders have special authority to interpret Scripture, so I take as my guide for life both the word of Scripture and the teaching of the Church.'

(c) 'There are two parts to the Bible: the Old Testament and the New Testament. The Old Testament is a Jewish book, and although it has some relevance for Christians, I feel that the New Testament, especially the teaching of Jesus, has more authority.'

(d) 'The Bible is a collection of books written over hundreds of years. The people who wrote these books did have special insights, but being human they could never come to more than a partial understanding of the truth. The Bible may be a guide to behaviour, but it is not infallible. I also believe that God did not cease to reveal his will to people in the second century AD. There have been many people over the past two thousand years who have been inspired by God, and I trust the judgement of many of them as much as that of the Biblical writers.'

(e) 'The Bible contains the teaching of men, not of God. It was written a long time ago for a very different society, and has very little relevance for people living in the twentieth century. In matters of behaviour, everyone must follow their own conscience.'

---

**Something to discuss and write about**

1 Why do some people say that Church leaders should be better able to interpret the Bible than other people? Do you agree with this point of view?

2 Why do so many Christians regard the teaching of Jesus as binding on their lives? (John 8:28)

3 Why is it sometimes believed that some people are closer to God than others and are better able to understand his will?

4 Can you name any people in post-Biblical times who have been regarded as great authorities on religious matters, or who have set a Christian example which others might wish to follow?

5 What do you understand by the word 'conscience'?

6 Do you think that your conscience is a reliable guide?

7 Are there any dangers in relying only on your conscience when you make decisions?

8 Does 'obeying your conscience' mean any more than 'doing what you like'?

---

## Solving modern problems

When you were discussing the use of the Bible, you may have decided that one difficulty in looking to the Bible for answers to every one of life's problems is that many situations which occur in our lives were totally unheard of then. In fact, the majority of the topics in this book fall under that heading. There is nothing in the Bible directly related to endangered species, nuclear weapons or medical ethics. The same problem occurs for people of other faiths whose Scriptures also date back many centuries. Religious people have a number of options open to them when making up their minds on current issues. Consider the following suggestions and discuss them. Can you think of any others?

1 'I want to follow the traditional teaching of my religion in the running of my life. Since my Scriptures say nothing about the use of life-support machines I will simply ignore the subject.'

2 'My religion does not say anything about the use of nuclear weapons. Therefore I feel that I can make my mind up on this subject without reference to my religious belief.'

3 'My Scriptures do not say anything about the use of contraceptives, but it is the official teaching of my religion that artificial methods of birth control may not be used.'

4 'The Scriptures of my religion say nothing about race relations. However, since I want to live according to the spirit of my religion, I must work out an attitude towards race relations which I feel is in harmony with the teaching of my Scriptures on other matters.'

## Authority and free will in Christianity

People who are not religious often get the impression that religion, especially Christianity, is one big 'Thou Shalt Not'. In fact one of the difficulties of being a Christian is that some Churches do *not* lay down hard and fast rules which must be kept. On the other hand in some Churches the priest or minister tells the congregation exactly what to think – tells them what is right and wrong. After all, some people like to be told. It may make them feel safe and secure: they know where they stand. But there are also ministers who leave their congregations to draw their own conclusions and even challenge the official teaching of the Church. Some people find this very threatening, but others find that it is a great relief to have someone in authority tell them that their salvation does not depend on their believing in, for instance, the virgin birth of Jesus.

---

### Research and discussion

Find out about:
(a) The popular writings of Bishop John Robinson (then Bishop of Woolwich) in the 1960s.
(b) Some of the statements of the Bishop of Durham in and after 1984.
  Do you think that people who state such opinions openly should not be allowed to hold office in the Church?

The expression 'free will' has already been used in this book. Find out what it means. Now try to answer these questions and see if they bring you any nearer to understanding the concept of free will.
1 If God created us good, why do we do evil things?
2 What would people be like if every time a person was about to do something which would hurt others, God stopped them from doing it?

---

### The law of love for Christians

'Love' is a word used a great deal by Christians. Jesus did not lay down a large number of regulations to be followed at all times. You will probably have discovered that, according to Jesus, there were two great commandments which summed up all the others. 'Love the Lord your God, and your neighbour as yourself' (Matt.22). In St John's Gospel we find something similar: 'I give you a new commandment; love one another; as I have loved you, so you are to love one another. If there is love among you, then all men will know that you are my disciples.' (John 13:34)

It would seem then that Jesus wished above all for a 'loving' attitude to be found among his followers. So perhaps we should go on now to ask: Can we say that loving God and loving our fellow human beings is a good basis of Christian behaviour?

---

### Something to discuss and write about

1 What do you think Jesus meant by 'love' in the way he used the word? Can you think of other words which might have a similar meaning?

---

*continued*

2 How do you decide what is the loving thing to do in any given situation?
3 Think of occasions when by acting out of love you might be offending others or even breaking the law.
4 Supposing that you have to decide between two courses of action, both of which could be the right thing to do under the circumstances. How do you decide which option to take?

Here is an example: A school has two conflicting rules: 'Always pick up litter' and 'Do not walk on the grass'. What do you do if you see litter in the middle of the lawn? Or: a vicar finds a burglar in his front room. The law would have the vicar call the police who would then take the burglar to court, but his religion tells him not to condemn others, and always to forgive. What should he do?

See if you can think of any other situations like these where the same problems arise, and give them to your friends to work out.

You may have decided by now that although working through moral problems can be interesting in theory, in practice you have a lot of sympathy with the girl mentioned in the Preface who said that if she spent her whole life thinking about what was the right thing to do, she would never get anything done! We began this chapter by asking on what basis a religious person might try to form a personal code of conduct. We have noticed the following points:

1 Some religious people base their morality heavily on the teaching of their sacred texts.
2 Some obey the teachings of their religious leaders.
3 Some regard their behaviour as a matter for their own conscience.
4 On many issues others may not make any conscious judgement at all, because certain types of behaviour are accepted by our society and others are rejected. Most of us are brought up to accept certain rules without question.

## Knowing your mind

### Something to discuss and write about

Many people think that it is important that we all have a code of behaviour, that is, a set of principles on which we base our actions. Here are some of the reasons given for holding this point of view. Give your own opinion on each of these statements.

1 If no one acted on principle, we would all do what suited us best in any given situation. The result would be a selfish and disorganised society.
2 People who live in countries with elected governments have the ability to vote for and against certain policies. Political parties have policies on matters such as nuclear weapons, overseas aid and capital

punishment. We should all be able to make decisions on such issues on a sounder basis than simply whether we like it or not.

3 Many people, such as doctors and lawyers, have to make difficult decisions which affect the welfare and happiness of others. Their judgements should not be based on their own whims, but should be made with reference to a wider code of conduct or set of beliefs which have stood the test of time.

4 Our generation must constantly be making new laws for the smooth running of society in the future, just as rules which make our society run smoothly were made in the past. If the people who make these rules simply act on what suits them best, the rules they make are not likely to be very satisfactory for other people.

5 On the other hand we need to be able to argue against some actions and regulations which we believe are wrong. This sort of dispute is fairly common in the area of traffic laws. When the law making the wearing of crash helmets compulsory for all motor cyclists was introduced, there were protests from the Sikh community. By wearing a crash helmet, Sikh men would have to break the religious law which required them to wear a turban. On another occasion many people objected to the compulsory introduction of seat belts on the grounds that it interfered with human liberty. The reason why the protesters in both cases made the headlines was that they could produce arguments based on sound reason deriving from their beliefs, in one case religious, and in the other humanitarian. If the objectors had simply said of the new laws, 'I don't like it', probably no one would have taken any notice of them. Try to think of any other individuals or groups who have made a serious impact on the thinking of other people because their arguments have been so impressive.

# 2 The world around us

We all know people who have authority and power. Sometimes they wear a uniform, to show that they are in the police force, or are a traffic warden, for example. They may wear a badge saying 'Prefect', 'Captain' or 'Librarian'. Some of these people want power for its own sake, because ordering people around gives them a feeling of superiority. Some want power so that they can manipulate others, or make a profit out of them. But many people regard the possession of power as a serious responsibility, like that of a parent. A mother has responsibility for her child, and will use this authority to love and protect it. Jesus once spoke to his disciples about 'masters' and 'servants' (John 13), and he, like a servant, washed their feet as an example of how a master should behave. Unlike the 'kings of the earth' he did not wish to 'lord it over them'.

The entire human race has been given a great authority – the responsibility to determine the fate of the planet which is our home. The actual power has fallen into the hands of a few, but we all have a responsibility to influence the way they use it. Like anyone else with authority we can either say, 'All this is mine and I'm going to use it for my own advantage and get whatever I can out of it'; or we can say, 'I am in a position to do great harm or good. I must act responsibly to make sure that all living things are cared for and that all are fairly treated.'

The idea in the Western world that the human race is superior to the rest of creation is rooted in the book of Genesis in the Old Testament.

> God said, 'I give you all plants that bear seed everywhere on earth and every tree bearing fruit which yields seed. They shall be yours for food.'  (Gen.1:29)

> 'The fear and dread of you shall fall upon all wild animals on earth, all birds of heaven, on everything that moves upon the ground, and all fish in the sea; they are given into your hands.'  (Gen.9:2)

## Religion and conservation

Science and technology have made tremendous strides during the last century. But over the past thirty or forty years, many people have begun to realise that what was thought of as progress for the human race, has in fact only been progress for some; and this progress has often been at the expense of other human beings and of other species which have suffered or even been destroyed in the process. In our rush to take whatever will improve our material standard of living, are we losing our respect and sense of wonder for the created order? Are we seeing the planet as something which exists purely for our convenience, in which other species just happen to live?

A great sense of wonder at the beauty of creation was expressed in the Old Testament in the poems and songs called the Psalms.

The heavens tell out the glory of God,
the vault of heaven reveals his handiwork.
One day speaks to another,
night with night shares its knowledge,
and this without speech or language,
or the sound of any voice.
Their music goes out throughout all the Earth,
Their words reach to the end of the Earth.
(Ps.19:1–4)

**Research**
What ideas about God, the human race, the world and nature do you find
in the following Psalms?
    8; 65:9–13; 95:1–7; 104; 148.

*Buddhist ideas about the world*
Many Buddhists are highly critical of the idea found in Judaism and
Christianity that the human race is especially appointed by God to be
in command of nature. The assumption that we are superior to the
rest of nature has led us to exploit this planet and other species on it.
    Buddhists think of the human race as being in harmony with
nature, and part of it rather than lord over it.

We speak as though man and
Nature do not belong to the
same reality. In Chinese water
and ink paintings much space is
always given to Nature, and
man is included as part of
Nature. . . . Man is an animal,
part of Nature. But he has
singled himself out from the rest
of Nature, as if he himself were
not part of it. He then poses the
question, 'How should I deal
with Nature?' Why, man should
deal with Nature the way he
should deal with himself! He
should not harm himself, he
should not harm Nature. . . . If
he knew how to deal with
himself, and with his fellow
humans, he would know how to
deal with Nature. A person,
human-kind, and Nature, are
inseparable. Therefore by not
caring properly for one of these
three, man harms all three.
            (Tich Nhat Hahn, from
                *Down by the Riverside*,
            Buddhist Peace Fellowship,
                Summer–Autumn 1984)

### Hindu ideas about the world

Hindu tradition teaches about a 'wheel' of life, a never-ending cycle of creation, preservation and destruction. Over and above all things is the Supreme One, and all living things are filled with a part of his power. The Hindu also believes that all living things have a soul, and that this soul will be born many times before it can finally return to the Supreme One. This means that to the Hindu, as to the Buddhist, all living things are important in the cycle of life. As a result, many Indians are vegetarian. The fact that most Indian restaurants in Britain (even those run by Hindus rather than Muslims) serve mainly meat meals, is a reflection of Western rather than Indian habits. The belief is that since many other sorts of nutritious food are available to us, there is no need to kill animals for their meat.

### Jewish ideas about the world

Even if few Jews today believe in the Creation Story in Genesis as a historical account, many do believe in the ideas about God and the human race that appear in the story. The story says that the earth was created for the benefit of people. So, many Jewish traditions and festivals are connected with the harvests, and thank God for providing for people. On the other hand, they believe that people have been given a great responsibility to care for the earth, and must not misuse it.

### Muslim ideas about the world

Muslims also believe that the human race was the greatest of God's creations. Jews, Christians and Muslims share similar Creation traditions, and not surprisingly their traditional beliefs about the care of the Earth are quite similar. Islam began in countries where drought and famine were not uncommon, and there is a great stress in Muslim teaching that waste of resources is wrong. Most Muslims do not approve of hunting animals for sport, since this is a waste of life, and many do not approve of zoos or circuses. So Islam, too, demands that people care for the Earth and do not misuse it.

---

**Research**

Ask members of your group who are studying Geography to talk about ecosystems and to explain why it is so important that ecosystems are preserved.

---

### The words of a 'savage'

In 1854 the United States government offered to buy a large area of land from the Indians. Chief Seattle was one of the great chiefs in the area, and he gave this reply to the offer:

How can you buy or sell the sky, the warmth of the land? The idea is strange to us. If we do not own the freshness of the air and the sparkle of the water, how can you buy them? Every part of this earth is sacred to my people.... The white man's dead forget the country of their birth when they go to walk among the stars. Our dead never forget this beautiful Earth, for it is the mother of the red man. We are part of the earth, and it is part of us. The perfumed flowers are our sisters; the deer, the horse, the great eagle, these are our brothers. The rocky crests, the juices of the meadows, the beauty of the pony, and man – all belong to the same family.

... The water's murmur is the voice of my father's father. The rivers are our brothers, they quench our thirst.... If we sell you our land, you must remember and teach your children that the rivers are our brothers, and yours, and you must henceforth give the rivers the kindness you would give to any brother.

We know that the white man does not understand our ways. One portion of the land is the same to him as the next.... The Earth is not his brother but his enemy, and when he has conquered, he moves on.... He treats his mother the earth, and his brother the sky, as things to be bought, plundered and sold.... If we decide to accept (your offer) I will make one condition: the white man must treat the beasts of this land as his brothers. I am a savage, and do not understand any other way. I have seen thousands of rotting buffaloes on the prairie, left by the white man who shot them from a passing train. I am a savage and cannot understand how the smoking iron horse can be more important than the buffalo that we kill only to stay alive. What is man without the beasts? If all the beasts were gone, man would die from a great loneliness of spirit.

... This we know, All things are connected like the blood which unites one family. Whatever befalls the earth befalls the sons of the earth. Man did not weave the web of life, he is simply one strand in it. Whatever he does to the web, he does to himself.

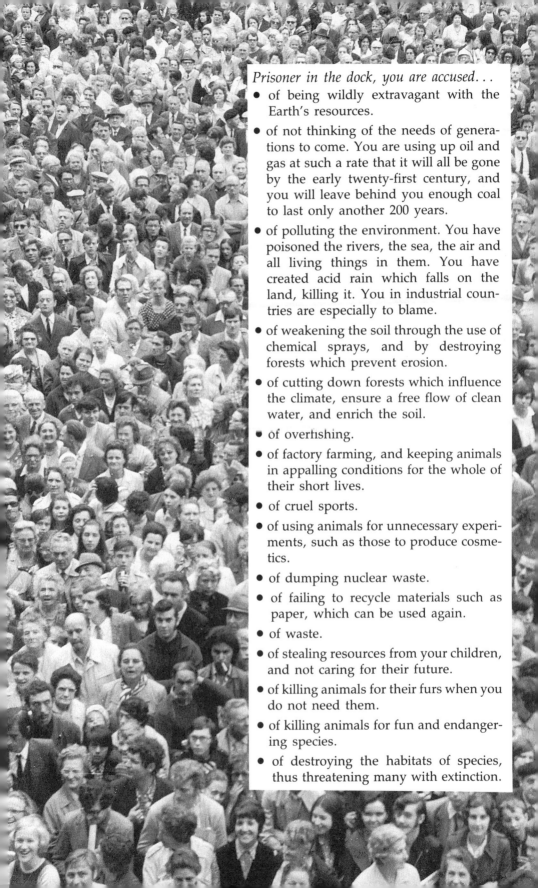

*Prisoner in the dock, you are accused...*

- of being wildly extravagant with the Earth's resources.

- of not thinking of the needs of generations to come. You are using up oil and gas at such a rate that it will all be gone by the early twenty-first century, and you will leave behind you enough coal to last only another 200 years.

- of polluting the environment. You have poisoned the rivers, the sea, the air and all living things in them. You have created acid rain which falls on the land, killing it. You in industrial countries are especially to blame.

- of weakening the soil through the use of chemical sprays, and by destroying forests which prevent erosion.

- of cutting down forests which influence the climate, ensure a free flow of clean water, and enrich the soil.

- of overfishing.

- of factory farming, and keeping animals in appalling conditions for the whole of their short lives.

- of cruel sports.

- of using animals for unnecessary experiments, such as those to produce cosmetics.

- of dumping nuclear waste.

- of failing to recycle materials such as paper, which can be used again.

- of waste.

- of stealing resources from your children, and not caring for their future.

- of killing animals for their furs when you do not need them.

- of killing animals for fun and endangering species.

- of destroying the habitats of species, thus threatening many with extinction.

**Something to discuss and write about**

1 Read the list of accusations against the human race. Which, if any, do you think are fair? Give reasons for your answers.
2 What do you think would be the attitude towards these issues of people belonging to any of the religions you have studied?
3 As a group, try to find at least one illustration from books and newspapers of each 'accusation', e.g. you may find an article on an animal which is threatened with extinction.

## Religion and wealth

*Judaism*

Traditionally, Jewish teaching took an approach to wealth which people believed would, if it worked in practice, produce a just society.

The Tenach (the Jewish name for what Christians know as the Old Testament) teaches that God created the world and it was good. The material things of the world were given for all living things to enjoy, including the human race. So Judaism does not condemn the possession of wealth and riches since such things are seen as a gift from God.

It was always obvious that the wealth of the world was not distributed equally between all people. In traditional Jewish teaching this is not regarded as wrong. Material prosperity, it was often taught, is a reward from God for those who are faithful to him.

However, Jewish teaching does not regard ownership as absolute in the sense that people may do as they wish with their property. The owner of, say, a piece of land, is looking after it on God's behalf. He or she is God's steward and the land is his sacred trust.

Both the Tenach and the Talmud (the books of Jewish law based on the Tenach) assume that the poor have a *right* to share in the good things of the earth. They may not have been chosen to administer the world's wealth, but they have an equal right to share in it. The 'stewards' who do administer it have a great responsibility to see that it is administered for the good of all. If some people are more highly favoured in this world, it simply means that they have a greater responsibility and a greater opportunity for administering justice.

So, caring for the poor has always been an obligation for the Jews. In the Tenach there are laws which say that a portion of the harvest should be given to those with no land. The Talmud insists that giving money, food and clothing is a duty. There is no question of discussing whether you can afford it, or whether you should look after your own needs first. A person gives to the poor, not out of kindness of heart, but because the poor have a right to receive their share. The

Talmud also encourages Jews to lend money to those without the means to support themselves so that they can set up a business. However, the person who lends money has a duty to see that it is being spent wisely – that is, that it is being spent in a way that will improve the standard of living of the borrower. Idleness, beggary and scrounging are not encouraged!

All this should help to explain why the prophets in the Tenach were so outspoken against the rich who 'trampled the poor into the ground'. It was not because they were rich that they were condemned, but because they did not fulfil their obligations to the poor. The duties of the rich and powerful are expressed in this way in one of the Psalms:

> God takes his stand in the court of heaven to deliver judgement.
> How long will you judge unjustly and show favour to the wicked? You ought to give judgement to the weak and the orphan, and see right done to the destitute and the downtrodden; you ought to rescue the weak and the poor and save them from the clutches of wicked men.    (Ps.82: 1–4)

### Christianity

The matter of wealth is an important one in the New Testament. Christianity has inherited the Jewish teaching on wealth found in the Old Testament, and has taken up the cry of the prophets for justice for the poor. However, although there have always been people in the Church who have accepted the Jewish idea that wealth is a gift from God to be enjoyed, there have also been those who have denounced the possession of wealth for Christians. The monastic movement has always, in theory at least, adopted poverty as one of its principles, even though in the Middle Ages many monasteries were very rich. There have always been Christians who have claimed to be following the teaching of Christ in saying that private ownership of property is wrong. They say that Christians should not give to the poor from a position of financial superiority, but that they should identify with the poor by selling all they have, like the apostle Barnabas, and become poor themselves. The Church has never been united over the issue of money, and this unease continues today with many Christians being critical of the wealth of the established Churches in an age when poverty and starvation are worldwide problems. It is also a matter of embarrassment for some Christians that the power-base for the Church is still in the rich countries of Europe and North America.

> ### Passages for discussion
> Here are some passages from the Bible. Some are from the Old Testament and so are relevant for both Judaism and Christianity. Some are from the New Testament. Discuss these questions and any others which you think arise from the passages concerned.

1 Amos, chapter 4. (Amos lived in the eighth century BC.) Are there any ways in which you think Amos's Israelite society pictured here was like our own today?

2 Amos 5:11–13.
- (a) Find four ways in which the poor in Amos's time were disadvantaged.
- (b) What do you think Amos meant when he said, 'A prudent man will keep quiet'? Is it likely that people today 'keep quiet' under the same conditions and for the same reasons?

3 Matthew 25:31; Luke 16:33–6. Do you believe that we will be judged by God according to our behaviour towards those who are worse off than ourselves? If not, what other reasons are there why we should give aid to those who are poorer than we are?

4 What do the following passages say about Christians and wealth? *Can* a rich person be a true follower of Jesus?
Matthew 5:19–34; 19:16–26; Luke 1:53; 1 Timothy 6; James 5:1–6.

5 What solution did the earliest Christians find to the problem of poverty and wealth? (Acts 4:32–6)

What problems do you think there would be for twentieth-century Christians trying to follow their example? Try to find out about any Christians who have tried to live like this.

## Islam

Many Muslims share the view we have already found in Christian and Jewish thinking that the human race are trustees, or guardians of the Earth. The real owner is God.

A fundamental principle of Islam is Zakat (meaning 'purity'). Zakat is almsgiving. This means that richer members of the community share their wealth with the poor. Islam teaches that all people are precious to God, whatever their position in society, and that the poor have a right to assistance.

The payment of Zakat (pictured below) varies from country to country. In countries which are governed by Islamic law, Zakat is more or less compulsory on those who can afford it at a rate of 2½%

per year of their total wealth. But in countries like Britain the payment of Zakat is voluntary and there is no fixed percentage. In Britain, local mosques usually supervise the collection of Zakat and distribute the money to where it is needed.

Zakat is not a purely social convention to help the poor, but is a religious duty, and for many a privilege. It is seen by the wealthy as a means of purification, and when it is given in the right spirit – that is, as a means of showing one's gratitude to God and of doing good – it is a form of worship.

We have seen then that the three great Western religions all stress the need for sharing wealth, and all encourage generosity among their followers. Yet poverty remains an international problem. Before thinking any further of ways in which Christianity or any other religion can press for a greater degree of fairness in the distribution of wealth, we need to look at the actual problem, both at home and abroad.

## Poverty in Britain

Poverty is not something found only overseas. Of course all things are relative and the 'poor' in Britain are wealthy in comparison with the poor of the Third World. However, the problem is serious enough for people in the 1980s to be talking about Britain as 'two nations'. In 1985 there were 3½ million people unemployed and ¼ of the population earned so little that they paid no income tax.

Most, but not all, poverty in Britain is to be found in the inner cities. Poverty does not just mean lack of money, although this is obviously an important factor.

*Digging for coal on a slag heap.*

**Something to discuss**

*'Poverty is . . .'*

The following things have been described as marks of poverty in Britain. Do you think that this is the case? How can these things affect the quality of a person's life in this country?

- Poor housing
- Poor health
- Unemployment
- Living in an area with other poor families
- Depending on Social Security
- Not having a car
- Poor educational achievement
- High crime rate
- Being surrounded by pictures of wealth and consumer goods which you cannot afford.

Read the following descriptions of poverty then discuss them.

(a) They cut the gas off yesterday. I knew they would. We haven't had electric for six months now . . . . Yesterday I went to Social Security and Danny went down the tip. He goes there every day. He usually finds old furniture and stuff and we burn it. He found a pair of jeans there the other day that fit our Micky. He got a telly in March and made it work. He's clever like that. But we couldn't use it after they cut off the electric in April. I'm glad in a way. It's awful for the kids, especially Micky. He's not old enough to understand. He doesn't see why he can't have the things on the adverts. Once I saw an advert for some perfume, and I said without thinking, 'I'd love some of that.' Well, Micky went to Boots the next day and nicked some for me. Actually it was aftershave because he couldn't read the label, but it was a nice thought. No of course I don't want them growing up to be thieves. But Micky's only six. How can he understand? Everyone around here is like us. No one really bothers, do they? The Church? Don't be funny. We can't go to *church*. Me and Danny aren't married for a start. They'd throw us out, wouldn't they?

(*Excerpts from a recorded interview with Mandy*)

(b) A Liverpool policeman tells of just one incident on his rounds. We were watching them the other night, about half a dozen of them ripping away the plywood sheeting the Corporation had so kindly put over the disued shop. They were having immense fun pulling it off and smashing it to smithereens. Then they'd probably go inside and set light to the joint, you know, which is right underneath the flats where they live. And these kids were no older than my eldest, who's four.

(James McClure, *Spike Island*)

(c) This lad of 13 had done so many burglaries he doesn't care. First of all he was very hard . . . but when you get down and talk to him he's such a lovely little lad. Really and truly, deep down they're nice kids, but they just don't stand an earthly. By the time they're adults they're hard as nails.

It is very difficult for the very poor to improve their income. Families on low incomes can claim various allowances, but as soon as their weekly income rises, what they gain in income they lose in benefits and tax, so that they are usually only a few pence better off than they were. The name given to this situation is the 'poverty trap'.

*David Sheppard,
Anglican Bishop
of Liverpool.*

*How can the Church help the poor in Britain?*
Many people feel that the Church in Britain should be more out-spoken in defence of Britain's poor. With rising unemployment, help for the poor does not just mean financial help. The unemployed are often poor not just in terms of money but also in self-respect. Also they have been left with time on their hands. The following ideas have been put forward as to how the Churches can help the poor. What is your opinion of these ideas?
1 Many Church leaders are well-educated and influential people with powerful friends, both at national and local level. They should use their influence and contacts to make others aware of the situation of Britain's poor.
2 Many clergy these days have been specially trained to understand the problems of the inner cities where they work. They can encourage local people to build up their own communities and develop their self-respect by depending less on outside agencies to organise their lives.
3 Many of Britain's poor are black, or from white working-class families. These are the people who often regard the Church as a white middle-class establishment and not for people like them. The Church should be aware of the fact that it does not reach out to a large section of the population, and should look particularly at the sort of people who become priests and ministers. Most clergy still have a university degree or at least A-levels and come from middle-class families. It should be easier for people with few or no academic qualifications to become priests and ministers. This might attract to the job more people from areas which suffer from educational disadvantage.
4 Christians who live in prosperous areas where there is no sight of poverty can help in many ways.
  (a) If their church is wealthy they can offer loans for the unem-ployed to set up in business.
  (b) They can influence the attitudes of friends and colleagues.
  (c) Their church could pay for a local person in an area with a high poverty level to be trained as a priest or minister.
  (d) They can offer holidays for people who can't afford to leave the area where they live.
  (e) The richer Churches can form links with Churches in inner cities. Both can learn and benefit from the exchange.

**Greenfields – a debate**
Organise a class debate on the following issue between representatives of both pressure groups. Each group must state clearly the reasons for their point of view. Each member of the class should then write a letter to the council giving his or her opinion on the matter.

The borough of Larksborough is a predominantly middle-class area. At one end of the borough is Greenfields, a new private development made up largely of luxury flats and two- to four-bedroomed detached houses. At the other end of the borough is the Dickens Green Estate, a development of high-rise council flats built in the 1960s. Dickens Green has a reputation for problem families, vandalism and crime. A growing number of people on the estate are becoming unemployed. The children from Dickens Green go to a primary school built in 1940 to serve the estate.

Due to falling rolls, the Council has recently closed a junior school near the Greenfields development, and intends to sell the land to a developer who will build more private housing.

However, a pressure group is set up in the Borough led by a number of local clergymen. They want the Council to build council houses at Greenfields where some of the poorest-housed families from Dickens Green can be rehoused. When the Council appears to be listening seriously to this group, another committee is set up consisting largely of residents of Greenfields who do not want a council estate on their doorstep.

## Unemployment and the Church

One of the greatest causes of hardship in the 1980s has been, and will continue to be, unemployment. Many Churches have shown a great concern for the unemployed, and some bishops and clergy have, controversially, spoken out against government policies which they see as having given rise to such a high unemployment rate. A number of Churches have begun daytime schemes where the unemployed can get together for activities or just to talk, and one place where this has been done with great success is Truro. When we think of unemployment we tend to think of large inner-city areas, but in fact Cornwall has, out of the holiday season, one of the highest unemployment rates in the country.

St Paul's Church in Truro opened its crypt as a place for people to go in 1984. A number of 'workshops' operate in the crypt where people can go to develop their own particular interest. There is a theatre workshop. This does not aim to produce budding actors, but it does enable people to get the experience of working with others. Then there is a writers' workshop where people write about their experiences as a way of sharing them. There is a worrying growth in drug abuse throughout the country, and peaceful Cornwall is no exception. So a worker from an organisation which counsels drug addicts can also be found offering his services in the crypt of St Paul's.

The St Paul's project is financed by the Truro Council of Churches and by the Bishop Michael of St Germans fund which supports the Church Action for the Unemployed scheme.

The centre does not try to organise people, but to let them develop their own skills and interests. People go to St Paul's with their ideas, not to be told what to do.

---

**Suggestion for course work**

Find out about any schemes for the unemployed in your area in which religious organisations are playing a leading role.

---

### Rich and poor worlds

'This is your Captain speaking. On behalf of Transcontinental Airways, I hope that you are having a comfortable flight. You will be pleased to know that we are on schedule and in about ten minutes we will be entering the air-space of Nepal. If you look to the right you should get a good view of the Himalayas. The stewards and stewardesses will shortly be bringing you the lunch menu. I hope that you have an enjoyable meal.'

Catherine closed her eyes and remembered the last time she had been in Nepal. It was three months ago now. It had been the chance of a lifetime for 17-year-old Catherine when her grandfather, who had always been regarded as rather eccentric, had decided that she should broaden her very English education by 'seeing the world' while she was still young. He had paid for her ticket to Singapore where they had relatives, and she had stopped off to stay with her brother Stephen on the way. Now she was flying home from Singapore.

'What would you like for lunch, madam?' inquired the stewardess giving Catherine the menu card. She chose seafood cocktail, chicken in wine and a chocolate mousse to follow. Thirty thousand feet below, millions of Nepalese would, if they were lucky, be tucking into chillis, chapattis and beans or lentils, which was what they ate at every meal, every day. On special occasions they had rice, but that was a luxury.

'Wine, madam?' The stewardess was back. Catherine shuddered as she thought of what the people on the ground below her were drinking. She reached into her bag and took out the most treasured memory of her visit – a letter from Stephen to her sixth form friends back at school. Catherine had promised that she would give a talk on Nepal as soon as she returned, and Stephen had offered to make his contribution based on three years' experience in this, one of the poorest countries of the world. Stephen was working with a missionary society on a community health project in one of the poorest and remotest areas of the country. He had promised his mother that he would not take Catherine there, even though she had begged to be allowed to go.

Catherine re-read the beginning of Stephen's letter.

'Sixteen-year-olds in Nepal are about three-quarters of your size due to malnutrition and starvation. In fact they are lucky to be 16 at all, because many children die long before they reach that age. My next-door neighbour had twelve children when I arrived there. Now she has only one, a daughter, and she is dying. Sixteen-year-olds in Nepal do not go to school. Nor do the younger children. They have to work, tending the animals or digging and carrying stones. They have never heard of bicycles, computers or television. If they are really lucky they might have a pack of cards, but the greatest status symbol where I live is a watch. One man I knew earned enough to go to Katmandu and buy a watch. You'd think he'd bought a Rolls-Royce! But on the whole, people have nothing to do in their spare time – although they have very little spare time anyway. All their time is spent on trying to stay alive.

The people here wear the same torn woollen clothing all the year round, and they do not have shoes. The houses are made of mud and stone. Mine is too – and it leaks! I had two inches of rain in my house for two weeks. Everything was drenched. The women cook over open wood fires, and big wooden splints like matches are used for lighting. Most of the illnesses in my part of Nepal are due to respiratory problems caused by breathing in the smoke in unventilated rooms.

There is no clean water where I live, and even boiling it does not make it safe. There is no sanitation either. I dug a loo in my back

garden, but none of my visitors knew how to use it because they'd
never seen one before! Most people use rivers and streams. I don't
need to tell you the effect on the water! If you are thinking that these
people must be very ignorant, ask yourself how much you would
have known about personal hygiene if no one had told you about it.
A lot of Europeans here like myself are training women to be
community health workers. This often means no more than teaching
them how to dig a reliable sewage pit. That is free – a water-purifying
plant is not.

I haven't had a bath for months. Neither has anyone else around
here. For a start there aren't any baths, and secondly it would take
you the best part of the day to collect and burn the wood to heat your
water. On top of that you would walk a mile or so to fetch each load
of water. I know a little village near the Tibetan border where the
nearest water is 2000 feet below the village. That means that you have
to go down and up half the height of Ben Nevis just to collect your
water.

There is no transport here. Occasionally organisations like CMS
and VSO fly a small plane in with supplies, but on the whole
everyone walks. I walked to Katmandu last year. It took me seven-
teen days.

If you are ill you either get better or you die. There are no doctors,
dentists or medicines. Few people live over the age of 40 anyway.

A 16-year-old girl in Nepal will usually have at least one child and will have been married for six or seven years. She will work from 4 a.m. to 10 p.m. with her baby strapped to her back. She will collect firewood, mend the holes in the walls of the house, dig up stones, do the cooking. . . .'

'Your seafood cocktail, madam.' The difference 30 000 feet can make! Catherine put her letter away. Before she had gone to Nepal she had felt terribly important. *She* would come back and would tell them all about *her* experiences in the Third World. *She* would tell them what they ought to do about it. But now that she had been, she felt quite humbled by the experience – quite speechless. She didn't know where to start. Anything she could say on the subject would be such an understatement. She remembered the words Stephen had spoken to her one night:

'When I was a kid I was like all the others. I expected everything to fall into my lap – Christmas presents, birthday presents, pocket money, trips to the pictures or the seaside. I took it for granted that when I grew up I'd have decent food, a home of my own, a car, a good job. Now that I've been here, I'll never be able to look at England in the same way again. I've learnt that just to stay alive until the age of 30 is an achievement. Anything after that is a bonus! When I get home, if you ever hear me moaning about how little money I have, how awful my food is, what a lousy picture I'm getting on the TV – or anything else, just remind me of today. And I'll do the same to you! Just tell me that I'm privileged to be alive, and privileged to be in a position where I can come here and discover how lucky I am.'

---

### Something to discuss and write about

1 Work out how much water your family uses in an average day. What difference would it make to your lives if you had to walk a mile to fetch water and had no mains sewage?

2 Why do many people think that education is one of the most important things to improve in developing countries?

3 Why is education for girls especially important in countries like Nepal?

4 If you were to set up a school in Stephen's village, what subjects would you include in the curriculum?

5 What do you think makes someone like Stephen leave his comfortable life in Britain and go to work in Nepal? What might tempt you to do this yourself?

6 What difference do you think it will make to the lives of Stephen and Catherine to have lived in Nepal?

---

### Map work

You will need a duplicated map of the world and an atlas.

Colour the following areas *red*:

Europe, the USA, Canada, the USSR, New Zealand, Australia, Japan.

Colour the following areas *green*:

Africa, South America, Asia (except Japan).

What do you notice about the geographical location of the *red* and *green* areas? Draw a dotted line to separate the two areas.

You should now have a map which looks like the one in the Brandt Report. This document was produced out of concern for the wealth of the countries in the northern hemisphere compared with the poverty in the south. The Brandt Report emphasised that world development was not just a matter of giving aid to poor countries, but that all the countries of the world are interdependent. If the economy of the South suffers, the economy of the North will also. One of the famous slogans of the Brandt Report was 'You can't cut along the dotted line'. What do you think these words mean?

---

### Spot the difference

When you were younger, you probably had children's comics which contained picture quizzes where you had to spot the difference between two pictures. Here is a similar quiz, but the differences are more obvious. There are four sets of pictures here illustrating the contrasts between the richer and the poorer countries of the world. In each case, see how many differences you can find.

---

---

### Research

Diets in poorer countries often lack the following things. Find out the effects of not having enough:

(a) Protein     (c) Vitamin B     (e) Iron

(b) Vitamin A     (d) Vitamin D     (f) Iodine

## *FACTS ABOUT FOOD*

- One-third of the world's population eats one half of the world's food.
- In the North, people eat on average 25% more than they need.
- Meat and dairy cattle eat over 40% of the cereals we use.

## FARMING

Problems with food production in poorer countries:

1 Often the climate is poor and areas may suffer from floods or drought.

2 There is frequently a lack of machinery and fertilisers.

3 Many farmers cannot afford the transport needed to take their produce to market. Also there are few roads to the market towns from rural areas.

4 New strains of seeds are needed if a better crop is to be harvested.

# WATER

In 1984 there was a drought in Britain. David Penhaligan, MP for Truro, complained that people in his constituency were having to queue for water at standpipes. This was described as degrading.

- 1320 million people in the world do not have clean running water.
- 1730 million people in the world do not have efficient sanitation.

## EDUCATION

In 1948 the United Nations Charter of Human Rights declared that everyone has a right to education. In the South only ⅔ of children of primary school age are receiving education, and ⅓ of the 12–17 age-group.

## CHILDREN

There are an estimated 52 million child labourers in the world. They will have received little or no education; will have had few, if any, pets or toys; their parents have not been able to claim family allowance; they will have been sent out to school with little or no idea of what it is to be a child. They will soon grow old.

---

**Something to discuss and write about**

What can we do about it?
The following suggestions were made in the Brandt Report and elsewhere. Do you think that these are good suggestions as to how the North could help the South?

---

1 We should be prepared to give aid to countries which do not share our political views. If people are starving to death, they need help, and the political leanings of their governments are irrelevant.

2 We should give aid unconditionally. We should not expect the countries which receive aid to use the money to buy goods from developed countries or support their industry.

3 'Power is in the hands of the rich, and they use it to their own advantage' (Brandt). We should be prepared to give power to the poorer nations of the earth. (What sort of power do you think poor countries lack at the moment?)

4 John V. Taylor, Bishop of Winchester, wrote a book entitled *Enough is Enough*. Here are a few of his suggestions.

We should think whether we *need* what we buy.
We should not be led through the nose by advertising.
We should not waste food.
We should eat less meat.
Married couples should have two children – one their own and one adopted.
We should be prepared to pay a little more if necessary for products from Third World countries.

5 There are some companies which are notorious for exploiting their overseas workers by paying them very low wages. Christians and others concerned could (some do) buy shares in these companies and try to influence company policy at shareholders' meetings.

6 Governments have power. People who are concerned with world development should keep writing to their MPs and should form pressure groups in an attempt to influence government policy.

7 People who do not have much money can help the developing world by giving their time.

8 When we give aid, in the form of goods, teachers or machinery, we must be careful to consider the needs of the receiving country and not just give them goods which *we* think they need. We must give them things which support *their* way of life, and not necessarily those things which encourage them to accept *our* way of life.

9 We must work to curb the materialist outlook of our society. We must find other worthwhile things in life apart from possessions and money. 'We must look towards obtaining personal satisfaction and fulfilment in ways that are less materially extravagant.' (P. Marshall)

# A gift for the world's poor, the refugees and the disaster - victims through Christian Aid

The churches
in action
in relief
and
development

*Christians and aid*

Two of the best-known Christian relief agencies are Christian Aid and the Catholic Fund for Overseas Development (CAFOD).

Like all other agencies they are concerned both with short-term emergency relief and long-term development. Emergency relief is given in times of crisis, such as when the terrible famine hit Ethiopia and other parts of Africa in 1984–5. Although emergency relief may help save lives in the short term, it is no answer to the long-term problems of developing nations.

The aim of these organisations is to help countries stand on their own feet and be able to take control of their own development. We saw that the Brandt Report also took this view. But if poor countries are to develop, we in the North must be prepared to make some concessions; for example, we must be prepared to loosen our stranglehold on world trade.

There is no one Christian attitude to aid. Some Christians believe that it is their 'duty' to give charity to the poor, but that Christians should not get involved with political action. Others, however, say that the only way to help the poor, both at home and abroad, is to change the structures of society and the international dealings which result in poverty. This was recognised by the Second Vatican Council which set up CAFOD:

'Not only the effects but also the causes of various ills must be removed. Help should be given in such a way that the recipients may gradually be freed from dependence on others and become self-reliant.' (Vatican II)

---

*'In every human being in need we are confronted by Jesus Christ himself and . . . if we deny him in this encounter, we cannot belong to him.'*
(Christian Aid statement)

---

*Liberation theology*

Liberation theology began in South America and challenges many of
the traditional Christian ideas developed among the white and
comparatively wealthy Christians of Europe. In South America
Catholic priests work alongside their parishioners in appalling conditions of poverty and oppression, where they run a risk of being
abducted or shot by the police, as was Father Jarlan in Santiago in
Chile in Summer 1984. Liberation theology sees the poor as the
Church's first priority. For centuries rich Christians have ruled the
Christian world while the poor lacked not only money but also a
dignified standard of living. They do not have the chance to take part
in the government of their own countries, and their women in
particular lack status and power.

Liberation theology takes its ideas from Jesus himself. When he began his ministry he quoted from Isaiah:

'The spirit of the Lord has appointed me; he has anointed me; he has sent me to announce good news to the poor, to proclaim release for prisoners and recovery of sight for the blind.'   (Luke 4:18)

When John the Baptist asked if Jesus was the one to come (i.e. the Messiah), Jesus answered, 'Tell John what you have seen and heard. The blind recover their sight, the lame walk . . . the deaf hear . . . and the poor are hearing the good news.'   (Luke 7:22)

Also Mary, when she heard that she was to be the mother of the Saviour, said 'he has filled the hungry with good things and the rich he has sent empty away'.

When the Catholic Bishops in Latin America held a conference in Pueblo, Mexico in 1979, they stated that certain courses of action had to be taken.

1 The conference said that the extremes of poverty in South America were contrary to the spirit of the Gospel.
2 The bishops denounced the system which had given rise to such poverty.
3 They said that they wanted to work with other Churches to create a world of greater justice and brotherhood.
4 They said that local cultures should be encouraged and respected.

Many Catholics and members of different Christian groups sympathise with the teachings of liberation theology, but feel that it is 'too political'. To many Christians, liberation theology looks like Marxism, and there are indeed similarities between the two ways of thinking. The question is, can a Christian sympathise with Marxist teaching?

'Christians cannot be silent when confronted by an unjust society. If they are, they condone it, and when they do so unconsciously, they are real sinners.'   (Cardinal Aloisio Lorscheider)

In 1984 Fr Leonardo Boff, a Brazilian Franciscan, was summoned to Rome to account for his views. Here are some of his ideas.

1 The Church in South America and elsewhere has kept up its position by supporting corrupt governments. The Church has always associated with the rich and the ruling classes and has given charity to the poor without seriously trying to change their position.
2 Local Churches should be free to make their own decisions. They should not have to take orders from Rome.

On a visit to South America in 1979 Pope Paul VI made his views clear:

> The Pope loves you because you are those whom God especially loves. He himself when he was founding his family the Church, was mindful of the poor and needy so as to redeem them. And that is exactly why he sent his son, who was born and lived among the poor so as to make them rich in their poverty.

> (Address at Pueblo 1979)

### Something to discuss and write about

1 'Salvation concerns the whole being; his health, education, and the dignity of his life' (Archbishop Avelar of Salvador). 'I feel that the revolutionary struggle is a Christian and Priestly struggle' (Camilo Torres). In what situations might it be right for Christians to try to change society by revolutionary means? (See chapter 6.)

2 Christians who teach liberation theology believe that Jesus did not mean his followers to give to the poor from a position of greater wealth, but that he intended them to become poor themselves. What do you consider to be the New Testament evidence for and against this point of view?

3 St Paul (1 Corinthians 7:29–31) said that it is easier for an unmarried person to live in poverty because he or she has no family responsibilities. What do you think were his reasons for saying this? Would it be reasonable for a whole family to choose to live the poverty of the poor or should adults who wish to live this sort of life not impose it on their husbands, wives and children?

# 3 Other races and religions

*Ebony and ivory, live together in perfect harmony ...*

So begins a famous song by Paul McCartney and Stevie Wonder, one a white singer, the other black.

They were not the first people to see the piano with its black and white keys as a symbol of our multi-racial community, where ideally black and white people can also 'live together in perfect harmony'. When you play only the white notes on a piano, or only black notes, there are not many works that you can perform. It is only when all the notes are used that the musician gets the full value and richness out of the instrument.

So it is with our society. It can only work well and give of its best when people of all races and colours work together and learn from each other, but without anyone losing their distinctive identity and culture.

However, there are many difficulties in the way of a happy, integrated society, not only in Britain but in many other parts of the world. The most powerful countries in the world, not only politically but also economically, are largely white. White people hold most of the financial power in the world; white countries are prosperous. Have you ever seen pictures of starving *white* people in the Third World?

That is not to say that all black people or black nations are without influence, or live in poverty. But it is true to say that the scales are very unevenly balanced.

The same is true within individual countries. Britain and America, among others, have a poor record in their treatment of and attitudes towards black people. The ancestors of most black Americans of African descent were taken as slaves against their will. Britain on the other hand, although participating in the slave trade, concentrated on claiming overseas territories for herself and calling those territories

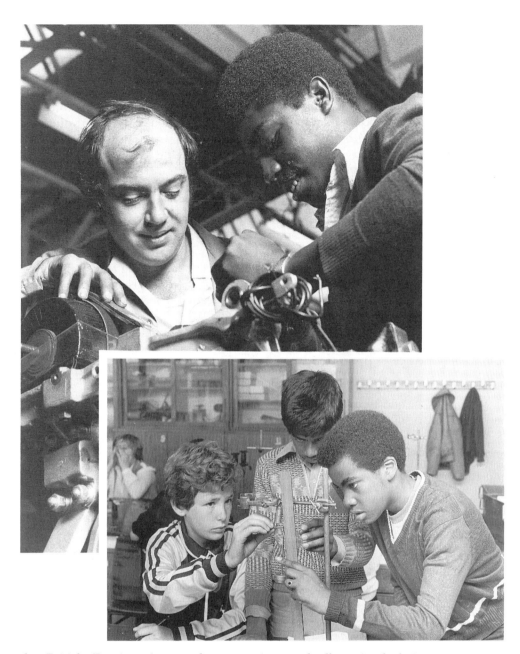

the British Empire. As member-countries gradually gained their independence they became part of the British Commonwealth, and their people were often given British citizenship, meaning that they had a right to settle in Britain. After the Second World War, when Britain was short of manpower, advertisements were placed in newspapers in the West Indies and the Indian sub-continent asking people to come and work in Britain. They came. But for many of them, the problems in their new home were as great as those they had left behind.

Britain has always been a place of refuge for people persecuted in their own lands, and there is a long tradition of immigration, as well as emigration. Yet many of the immigrants from the New Commonwealth and Pakistan have had more difficulty in being accepted by British society than have other immigrant groups. Why do you think this should be so?

## Personal prejudice

Prejudice, as the word suggests, means to pre-judge. A person who is prejudiced against another has made a judgement about them and formed an opinion without finding out any facts – in other words a prejudiced person is one who makes judgements out of ignorance.

Prejudice is very harmful because it often gives rise to violent emotions. One of the frightening things about trying to discuss with a prejudiced person the subject of their prejudice is the fact that they will not listen to reason – will not accept any facts which do not fit in with their existing ideas.

There are many forms of prejudice and none of us are totally free

from it. Some men are prejudiced against women; some women against men. Some are prejudiced against people from another social class, and some are prejudiced against people of a different race.

> **Something to discuss and write about**
> Which of the following factors do you consider to be causes of racial prejudice? Can you think of any others? Also, do you think that there is any truth in any of these fears and feelings?

1 *Slavery*. The ability of whites to make slaves of black Africans gave them a feeling of superiority.
2 *Immigration*. Black immigrants were originally settled in run-down areas of Britain's cities. People then began to accuse them of making these places unfit to live in.
3 *Territory*. Black immigrants were far more noticeable than white. This drew attention to them, and people began to be afraid that they were 'taking over the country'.
4 *Fear*. Black people brought new customs, religions, dress, food and language which were not understood. This made people afraid of the newcomers who appeared to be very different.
5 *Images*. White children may still grow up aware that their parents have few black friends, and that very few black people have authority over white people. But they also notice that white people often have authority over blacks. This may lead children to grow up with the idea of white superiority.
6 *Sticking together*. People from the same country who speak the same language and hold the same religion often prefer to live in the same areas. This sometimes makes it more difficult for different racial groups to get to know each other.
7 *In print*. Children's books have, until recently, assumed that Britain is white and middle-class. History books told stories of white conquerors. Everything in books about black people was negative.
8 *Threat*. Now that unemployment is becoming more of a problem, black people are seen by some as a threat to the jobs of white people.

*Acts and facts*
We sometimes hear white people say that black people are 'taking over'. These fears are often played on by organisations like the National Front and the British National Party. These organisations distribute free magazines, often delivered through letter boxes, which encourage hate and fear of black people. But now test your *knowledge* of the power and influence of black people, and immigration in general:

1 More people leave Britain each year than enter. *True or false?*
2 From what country does Britain's largest immigrant group come?

3 The total number of New Commonwealth citizens in Britain (belonging to a household where the head of the household is from the New Commonwealth) was in 1981 approximately: ½m.; 1m.; 2m.; 3m.; 4m.; 5m.; 6m.; 7m.; 8m.; more than 8m.?
4 As a proportion of the whole population of the UK, this was: 2%; 4%; 8%; 10%; 20%; 25%; 30%?
5 Here is a list of cities where immigrants from the New Commonwealth have settled. Put them in order according to which city you think has the highest proportion of black immigrants to the one which you think has the least. Have a guess at what percentage of the population is black in each case.

> Bristol   Leicester   Wolverhampton   Greater London
> Birmingham   Manchester   Sunderland   Bradford
> Liverpool

6 Britain is the only European country with black citizens. *True or false?*
7 In 1984 there were four black MPs in the House of Commons and two members of the House of Lords. *True or false?*
8 In the last three elections before 1985 the Conservative Party put up 1875 candidates: Labour 1871: Liberal 1713. In each case how many candidates do you think were black?
9 How many trade unions do you think had black officials in 1984?
10 How many Church of England and Catholic bishops in Britain are black?

(Answers on page 60)

---

**Research**

The statistics for the above questions date from the early 1980s. See if you can discover the most recent figures for at least some of these questions. Has the position of black people changed very much in recent years?

---

*Where Britain's immigrants come from*

*1981 Census*

Birthplace determined by that of the head of household.

| | | | |
|---|---|---|---|
| 48 290 586 | UK | 120 123 | Far East |
| 949 371 | Irish Republic | 170 178 | Mediterranean |
| 181 321 | E. Africa | 295 461 | Other N.C. |
| 545 744 | Caribbean | 1 313 129 | Rest of World |
| 64 561 | Bangladesh | | |
| 673 704 | India | | |

## Religion and race

### *Christianity and race*

It may seem that we have spent a long time studying facts and figures, and it may not be immediately obvious how this fits into a book about religious and moral attitudes. But if we are to form opinions, whether or not those opinions are based on religious convictions, we must be aware of the facts, otherwise we will simply not know what we are talking about. There is much more to learn on the subject and suggested reading will be found on pp. 154–5.

Christianity, Buddhism, Islam and to a certain extent Judaism, have all attracted believers from many different countries and races. In theory it might seem that religion could act as a unifying factor between races – something that is shared and held in common by people from all over the world. Unfortunately that is not always the case.

Christianity teaches that human beings are made in the image of God, and that all are equal in the sight of God. Jesus spent much of his time on earth with the people his society rejected, and many Christians today argue that a Church which does not share in Jesus' concern and care for *all* humanity cannot claim to follow Christ.

Colour prejudice is not an issue in the New Testament, but racial prejudice is. At the time of Jesus many Jews were prejudiced against non-Jews, or gentiles. This prejudice lived on in the early Church whose members were all, like Jesus himself, Jewish. Many of these Christians felt that the Church was for Jews aione, and it was only after a bitter argument that gentiles were admitted. In the light of this information, do you think that the following passages in the New Testament give any guidance as to what should be a Christian attitude towards racism and prejudice?

---

**Something to discuss and write about**
Read these passages from the New Testament and tackle the questions that follow.

---

1 Matthew 8:5–13.
 (a) What was the nationality of the centurion?
 (b) Why was it significant that Jesus helped him?
 (c) Why might some people have been shocked at what Jesus did?
2 Luke 17:11–19. Luke is thought to have been writing for gentiles and is the only evangelist to tell this story. What do you think he was trying to get his readers to understand from it?
3 Luke 10:25–37. Luke is the only evangelist to tell this story.
 (a) Who were the Samaritans?

(b) Why was it significant that the 'hero' of this story was a Samaritan?

(c) What do you think Jesus meant by saying, 'Go and do as he did'?

4 Acts chapter 10 (also written by Luke).

(a) What do you think was the meaning of Cornelius' dream?

(b) According to the story, who decided that Peter should baptise Cornelius?

(c) What did Peter learn from this whole experience?

5 Galatians 3:26–8. (St Paul)

6 1 John 4:17–21. What do you think the word 'brother' means here?

7 What do you think the following sayings of Jesus tell us about how he wanted his followers to behave towards other people?
Matt. 5:22; 7:1–5; Lk. 14:11; John 13:34–5.

### Islam and race

Many Muslims take a pride in their religion's lack of racial discrimination. Like Christianity, Islam attracts converts from all races and continents, but unlike Christianity there has never been a colour bar in its holy places: mosques or centres of pilgrimage. Malcolm X, the black power leader in the 1960s in America, once talked about the 'colour-blindness of the Muslim world.' Malcolm X believed that Islam could provide the religious and social basis of a multicultural society, and when visiting Makkah (Mecca) at the time of the Haj he wrote:

'Perhaps if white Americans could accept the oneness of God, then perhaps they could accept the oneness of man.'

### Judaism and race

In the opening chapters of the Tenach we find the statement that God made man in his own image. One of the beliefs in the Tenach is that all people are descended from the same ancestor, Adam, and that all men and women are in this sense brothers and sisters. The Board of Deputies of British Jews set up a working party on Race Relations in 1969. They knew that Jews can teach the world more than most about the terrible effects of racial hatred. This working party produced an important guide to new immigrants to Britain – not only Jews, but also those from the New Commonwealth. This guide aims to help new arrivals in Britain understand the structures of the society they have come into and gives general useful information.

## Racism

'Racism' and 'racist' are words we hear a lot today, especially in the inner cities. 'Racist' does not mean the same as 'prejudiced'. If we say that a society is racist, we mean that it puts people belonging to minority racial groups at a disadvantage. This *may* be done intentionally, out of prejudice, but it is often unintentional, and results from thoughtlessness rather than conscious discrimination. An example often used is that of school textbooks, which until recently used almost exclusively white people in their illustrations. This gave black people the impression that they were not regarded as full representatives of our society, and reinforced the idea that Britain was really a 'white' country.

## Institutional racism

When immigrants from the New Commonwealth first arrived in Britain, it was assumed that they would accept and adapt to the British way of life. No one seems to have thought that Britain might have to change if people from overseas were to stand a chance of creating a decent life for themselves.

Institutional racism in Britain is what puts black people at their greatest disadvantage. It means, not that people are intentionally racist (although they often are) but that the very laws, customs, traditions and policies of this country work on the assumption that everyone is white.

There are some fairly obvious examples of this.

1 A law was passed insisting that all motorcyclists should wear crash helmets. Sikhs felt that this discriminated against them because they could not wear crash helmets with their turbans. The law did not *mean* to discriminate against them – in fact the people who drew up the law probably did not even think of the Sikhs, which was half the trouble!

2 The average reading age of a claim form for family allowance has been estimated at 13–18: that of a trade union membership form about 17; and that of an Income tax return 15–18. This puts new immigrants with a limited knowledge of English at a disadvantage.

3 There are many jobs and apprenticeships which demand that applicants must have achieved certain qualifications by the age of 17 or 18. Many young black people who began their English education later in life *can* get these qualifications, but sometimes not by this age.

4 In the past many black children were regarded as unintelligent and were put in the lowest classes at school. Sometimes this assessment was made because their English, not their intelligence, was at fault. At other times black children had difficulty with so-called intelligence tests which asked questions like, 'What is the odd one out: Heathrow/ Harrow/ Gatwick/ Luton?' The answer is Harrow because it does not have an international airport, but how could a child recently arrived from India or Jamaica be supposed to know that? Again, the people who set these tests did not *intend* to discriminate against black children, they just did not think of them at all!

## Black and British

Many white attitudes in Britain, together with institutional racism, have led to black people being disadvantaged. Here are just a few of the problems of many black communities.

1 When the first immigrants arrived, it was in answer to British adverts in their local papers. In particular these were for jobs which white people did not want, especially in transport and hospitals. But during the 1960s, 1970s and 1980s, a series of increasingly severe immigration acts and regulations restricted the entry of black people into Britain. One of the reasons sometimes given for this is the decline in numbers of jobs, but this does not explain why white immigration is virtually unrestricted.

Meanwhile, black people already in Britain and their children found it difficult to move out of the low-grade jobs they were encouraged to come here to take. Research has shown that there is still a tendency for certain jobs to be regarded as 'black jobs'. It is still very difficult for most black people to get into 'white' jobs, or particularly for a black person to get a senior position over white people.

2 In the early 1980s the average weekly income for men was:

White £129 Asian £111 West Indian £109

Also black people have been the heaviest-hit by unemployment, and in some places a black person is three or four times more likely to be unemployed than a white person.

3 There is evidence that black children are often expected to do less well at school than white children, and are not pushed so much by teachers.

4 The latest report (1984) from the Policy Studies Institute shows that housing has always been a major problem. The first immigrants to arrive took mainly poorly-paid jobs in inner city areas, and were usually found cheap accommodation. Much of this was privately-owned and there were many scandals about overcrowding and appalling living conditions. A top priority for black families was to move, and West Indians especially wanted to move to council housing. But by the rules of most councils there were waiting lists, and black families were either at the bottom of the list, or, if their case was desperate, were sometimes given emergency accommodation – the lowest-quality accommodation kept for emergencies. It has proved very difficult for many West Indian families to get better council homes, sometimes, but not always, because of discrimination by housing officers.

## What black people think about it

In the end it doesn't matter that someone calls me a black bastard. What does matter is that my son has a fair chance of a good education, a good job and a decent place to live.          (A black priest in London)

Racism appears in the life of institutions – government departments, local councils, schools, industrial companies, trade unions, Churches and many others. Policies and practices assume that everyone is white.

('The Enemy Within', BCC)

White people don't know anything about us. All they know is that we beat up old women and things like that.                                 ('The Enemy Within')

Black people must reject everything the white man has said about him. Every sign and hint of racial superiority in the thinking of whites must be denounced by blacks. White men dragged the black man to this country [USA] against his will, stripped him of his African heritage, gave him a nondescript name, called him a Negro instead of an African, called him a boy instead of a man, rejected his racial characteristics, imposed a servile personality upon him and coerced him into believing he was inferior.

(A.M. Braxter, *Black Self-Determination*)

The white man has been my shepherd,
I shall always be in want.
He maketh me to lie down in the fields of poverty,
He despiseth my soul; he leadeth me into the field of human labour for his promise sake.
Yea when we toiled through the sea and cotton fields of death, he was doing no evil.
For he said his God was with him.
By whip and by chain he stampeth me.
He prepareth a table before me – on television – in the presence of my hungry children.
He anointeth my head with self-hatred and bitterness.
My cup runneth over.
Surely the fight for liberation and equality
Shall drive me all thee days of my life,
And I shall dwell in the house of freedom – some day.

(David Oden, *Journal of Christians and Politics*)

## The Church and racism

All the Churches in Britain have issued papers denouncing racism and pressing for racial harmony – but how much good has this done? Here is what one black Church of England priest has to say:

The Church of England is a racist organisation. All [except one] of the bishops are white and so are most of the clergy. Also representatives of the people or parish councils are mainly white and middle class. The black clergy (not only C. of E.) have recently formed an Association of Black Clergy. It is more likely that we will be heard as a group than as individuals. Of course a lot of people are leaving the Church of England because they find that they are not welcome there. I'm very worried because so few young blacks come forward for ordination. They don't see it as something for them. Yet if any of the Churches are to have any relevance and attraction for black people they must have black people among their leaders. The trouble is that black people have got so used to being dominated by whites that it's difficult for many of them to see themselves as leaders, and they have to be encouraged to do so. I am running conferences for young blacks thinking of ordination to encourage them.

I believe that those of us who are working to combat racism are not only seeking to liberate black people but also those whites who are held captive and are being degraded by their racist attitudes. They too need to be liberated from the racist attitudes they have inherited.

The Church of England appointed its first black bishop, Wilfred Wood, as Bishop of Croydon in 1985.

A black Roman Catholic priest from Trinidad comments on how he found England:

I came over from Trinidad three years ago to work with the Catholic Caribbean community in London.

Many West Indians find the churches in England cold and uninviting. We all know stories of black people who came here and automatically went to Anglican or Catholic churches because that's what they were used to at home. But in many cases they were politely told not to come again. Unbelievable, isn't it? I met someone only the other day who said that his priest has asked him to go to another church because his presence upset some of the white congregation. When you find that sort of attitude within the Church, you just want to give up.

I've travelled all over the world, and I forgot that I was black, just as you are not usually aware of being white. Your colour is something you just don't think about. But when I came to Britain I remembered. When I go around in my clerical collar it's different. People on the tube smile, and sometimes men raise their hats or shake hands, because I'm a clergyman. But when I wear ordinary clothes, I'm just another black. I was involved in a car crash at the traffic lights in Brixton once. A young white boy crashed the lights. A police car came screaming to a halt and the officer ignored the white boy but came straight to me and breathalysed me. And all the time I was breathing into the bag he was muttering abusive remarks in my direction.

---

### Something to discuss and write about

1 You have just read a number of statements and ideas written or spoken by black people. Make a list of the feelings which lie beneath these passages. Do you think all black people in Britain feel like this?

2 In what way can the Churches set an example by encouraging black people to take positions of leadership?

3 A number of the speakers suggested that the Churches are as racist as any other British institution. Does this shock you? Do you agree? How can the Churches try to change the attitudes of racist members?

4 The Church of England priest said that some white people are held captive by their racist attitudes. What do you think he meant?

5 The black Catholic priest found that people treated him differently according to whether or not he was wearing his clerical collar. Why do you think this happened?

---

One thing I know, which the white man may one day discover – our God is the same God. You may think now that you own him . . . but you cannot. He is the God of man, and his compassion is equal for the red man and the white.                                                    (Chief Seattle, 1854)

## Pentecostal churches and the black experience

Some black people attend the traditional British churches, but many, as we have seen, have been put off by the reception they received; many have found themselves more able to express their Christianity within the Pentecostal movement.

Pentecostal churches are noted for their happy, lively atmosphere. There is a lot of emphasis on individual response and participation, and on the giving of testimony by the 'brothers' and 'sisters'.

Worship is usually less organised than in traditional British churches, although Pentecostal ministers usually have considerable authority over their congregation, and often insist on high standards of morality, with a ban on tobacco, alcohol and drugs.

The black Churches have brought a new and lively approach to worship in Britain. But even before such Churches were established in this country, the black Christian movement had made one of its greatest contributions to Christian worship – through its music and poetry. It is ironic that the white slave-owners of America taught their slaves the religion which had as one of its Holy Books the Book of Exodus – the story of freedom for slaves! No wonder that many of the spirituals take the idea of the Exodus as their theme, such as in the song 'Go Down Moses'.

Some of these songs are deeply devotional, and they are used in many Church services today:

> Let us break bread together on our knees,
> Let us break bread together on our knees;
> When I fall on my knees with my face to the rising sun;
> O Lord have mercy on me.

Many others sing of the plight of the slave, and in looking forward with joy to a time of freedom, they speak for the oppressed people of all times and in all places.

> Nobody knows the trouble I see,
> Nobody knows but Jesus.
> Nobody knows the trouble I see:
> Glory Hallelujah!
> Sometimes I'm up, sometimes I'm down;
> O yes Lord;
> Sometimes I'm almost to the ground,
> O yes Lord.
> Nobody knows the trouble I see,
> Nobody knows but Jesus.

> Free at last, free at last;
> I thank God I'm free at last.
> on my knees when the light pass by;
> Thought my soul would rise and fly;
> I thank God I'm free at last.

*Who is this man?*
*Find out all you can about him.*

## Black theology

Black theology is an extension of liberation theology (see p 33). It is liberation theology applied to black people – Christian theology from a black person's point of view. The ideas behind black theology began in North America in the days when black and white Churches were segregated. (This was still the case in some places until quite recently.) Many black Americans were sure that the God of Moses and Exodus did not intend them to be second-class citizens.

Some black Christian teachers began to say that Christian theology had developed in 'white' European universities with white teachers. As one writer put it, 'Your God is too white.' One of the first teachers of black theology was James Crone, although his views are only some among many.

Crone said that Christian theology is about liberation (freedom). It is the story of how God set his people free from oppression. The story of the Exodus is a prime example of this. But even more than this, Jesus died to set us free. How can white people who keep blacks in a subservient position claim to be followers of Jesus?

Although black theology may seem aggressive at times, it also stresses reconciliation, and regards the coming together of black and white on equal terms as its ultimate goal. Black theology stresses that there is no equality until *all* are free. Racism holds white people captive as well – the captivity of their minds.

---

### Something to discuss and write about

*What can we do about racism?*
The Policy Studies Institute report of 1984 made a number of suggestions. They are listed below.
  (a)  In each case say whether you think these are good suggestions.
  (b)  How do you think these suggestions can be put into practice?

---

1  Black people must be given the opportunity of having better housing and better jobs.
2  Black people must be given good reason to trust the police force. At present many racial attacks against blacks are not reported.
3  Black and white must be able to live together without everyone losing their individual culture.
4  Landlords, employers and the police in particular must be made aware of discrimination in their areas and must be prepared to work against it.

### *What can the Church do about it?*

Christian communities have two assets at least which should make it possible for Christians to help get rid of racism. Firstly there are the huge buildings which can be used as a focal point in the community where meetings and cross-cultural activities can be held. Secondly the clergy as well as the laity are local people who are in a good position to be well informed about any problems in their area. Clergy are usually respected members of their community, and often have means of access to official circles where they can influence councils and institutions.

*The Community and Race Relations Unit*
The British Council of Churches represents all the British Churches working together in a number of areas. The Race Relations Unit has the following aims:

- to help Churches root out institutional racism from their structures.
- to issue booklets, audio-visual material, etc. to help Church members understand the issues involved.
- to pass on information about racism from the local Churches to government departments.
- to fund multiracial projects.
- to make constant approaches to the Government on
  humane and non-racist nationality laws
  deportations
  divided families

**Something to discuss and write about**
Try these questions, taking the appropriate column.

*Do people of many races live in your area?*

| YES | NO |
|---|---|
| 1 Ask black people you know to talk about any experiences they have of racism. | 1 Do you think that the problems of black people concern you? |
| 2 Does your school have an anti-racist policy? If so what does this policy say? | 2 How could people who live in rural areas or small towns with few if any black residents help to work against racism? |
| 3 How can you best respond to someone who is openly racist? (Remember that making them angry will probably only increase their prejudices.) | 3 Black people often complain that the 'black image' is often negative – for example most pictures of blacks show them in overcrowded cities, or starving overseas. The press seem to report stories about black muggers being arrested. Find out |
| 4 Many people believe that because black people have less chance than whites of getting good jobs, employers should sometimes practise *positive discrimination*. This means that some times black people should be given priority on principle. Do you think that this is a good idea? | about and discuss the work of black people who have made a positive contribution to many areas of life all over the world. (They are *not* all concerned with sport or pop music!) e.g. Sidney Poitier, Paul Robeson, Jessye Norman, Paul Boateng, Mrs Seacole, Leontine Price, Grace Jones, Daley Thompson. |

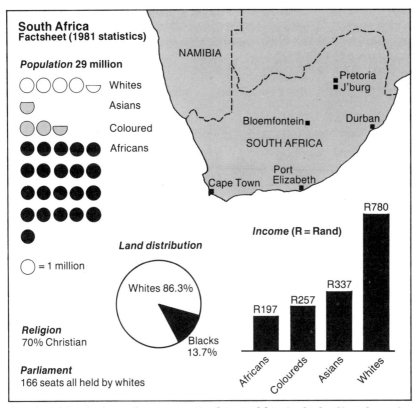

**South Africa**
Factsheet (1981 statistics)

*Population* 29 million

○○○○◡ Whites

◡ Asians

◐◐◡ Coloured

●●●●● Africans
●●●●●
●●●●●
●●●●●
●

○ = 1 million

*Land distribution*

Whites 86.3%

Blacks 13.7%

*Religion*
70% Christian

*Parliament*
166 seats all held by whites

NAMIBIA

Pretoria
J'burg

Bloemfontein

Durban

SOUTH AFRICA

Port Elizabeth

Cape Town

*Income (R = Rand)*

R780

R337

R257

R197

Africans  Coloureds  Asians  Whites

South Africa is the only country in the world to include directly racist policies in its laws and constitution. The law enforces a system called *apartheid* or separateness.

*Apartheid* in South Africa does not just mean that black and white communities develop separately, but that whites have nearly all the well-paid and powerful jobs in government and management, while blacks are forced to work as labourers in industry, in the mines or on farms, and most live in poverty. Forty-eight per cent of the 'African' population over the age of fifteen are illiterate, and not only are their opportunities for education restricted, but so are their rights of residence and freedom of movement. Blacks are forced to live in poor and overcrowded areas called tribal homelands, except for those blacks who are needed for work in and around the big cities. These workers are allowed to live in 'black' areas on the outskirts of the cities.

One of the most hated symbols of oppression for blacks are the Pass Laws which say that black people must always carry an identity pass containing all their personal details. A person who cannot produce the pass when a policeman asks to see it can be arrested at once. Also blacks can be arrested if they are caught in 'white' areas without permission. In any case they may only stay in these areas for 72 hours.

Some blacks are called 'migrant workers'. They are under contract, usually for a year, to work in 'white' areas, often as labourers in industry. However, since there is no attempt to give permits to relatives, families are frequently split up, since the workers are taken to live near their job, leaving the rest of the family in the homelands. They try to make a living through agriculture, but poor soil and lack of machinery lead to poverty and malnutrition.

In 1976 four of the tribal homelands were given a sort of independence with their own governments. However, the catch is that blacks living in the homelands have now been given the nationality of the homeland, and even blacks living in towns have been allotted to one of these homelands for their nationality. This has meant that millions of blacks have lost their South African citizenship. If the process continues there could in the end be no black South Africans.

## The Church and South Africa

South Africa is a Christian country, and for that reason, what goes on there must be of concern to other Christians in the world. About 40% of the whites belong to the Dutch Reformed Church which has, since the war, supported *apartheid*. It even has segregated Churches. This Church was expelled from the Association of Reformed Churches in 1982 for its racist policies. Not all white South Africans are in favour of *apartheid*, and some white Christians formed the Christian Institute which set out to fight the system. But the Institute was banned in 1977.

The leading organisation in the country against *apartheid* is the African National Congress, a multiracial organisation to which many Christians belong. This organisation has been traditionally opposed to violence, but in the early 1970s some members broke away to form a military wing, feeling that non-violence was not achieving anything. From the early 1970s the strongest Christian opposition to *apartheid* has come from the South African Council of Churches.

Many black South Africans do not belong to the established Churches but have set up their own Bible-based groups.

For some blacks, 'the Church in South Africa has been and continues to be part of the oppressive system. Christianity was used as a means to colonise, suppress and alienate the blacks' (Bishop Desmond Tutu).

Other blacks who remain committed Christians, 'rejected Christianity as projected by whites and their Church institutions. Going to Church and observing the cultic practices can no longer impress them as long as the Church is found wanting in the exercise of justice'.

(Bishop Mandlenkhosi Zuane of Swaziland)

## Bishop Desmond Tutu

Before 1984 some people had never heard of Desmond Tutu, Secretary of the South African Council of Churches. But suddenly his face appeared in newspapers all over the world, for in that year he was awarded the Nobel Peace Prize, and was also made Anglican Bishop of Johannesburg. Desmond Tutu did not regard the prize as something for him alone, but for 'all those who have been involved in the liberation struggle, working for a new society in South Africa.' The money that went with the prize is being used to finance a scholarship trust for young black people.

Desmond Tutu has always been an outspoken opponent of *apartheid*, and even when he had the opportunity, as a few blacks do, of living in the middle-class white area of Johannesburg, he refused, choosing instead to live with the black people in the township of Soweto outside the city. The Bishop has suffered harassment from the government on a number of occasions, and has had his passport confiscated. But he still supports the policy of non-violence, although he is in favour of civil disobedience – like defying deportation orders or going on protest marches. He sees this as part of his Christian witness: 'When I see injustice, I cannot keep quiet.' However, Bishop Tutu has warned that if a peaceful solution is to be found to the South African problem it must happen soon. Otherwise, he warns, there will be a bloodbath.

The following are some of his writings and speeches:

> There is probably just time for a reasonably peaceful resolution to the crisis
> . . . we are still holding out our hands of fellowship and saying to our
> white compatriots, 'grasp them – let us talk while there is still time'.

> The Christian must always be critical of all political systems, always testing
> them against God's standards.

> Christianity can never be a merely personal matter. It has public
> consequences and must make public choices. Many people think
> Christians should be neutral, or that the Church must be neutral. But in a
> situation of injustice and oppression such as we have in South Africa, not
> to choose to oppose, is in fact to have chosen to side with the powerful,
> with the exploiter, with the oppressor.

---

### Further Research
Find out about:

Nelson Mandela, Winnie Mandela, Steve Biko, Trevor Huddleston and more about Desmond Tutu.

---

### Something to discuss and write about
Many people think that the South African government will only change its policy if other countries put so much pressure on South Africa that its economy becomes seriously threatened, and the country becomes cut off from the rest of the world. Consider the following.

---

1 Would you:
   (a) refuse to buy South African produce in British shops?
   (b) refuse to deal with banks and companies which lend money to South Africa?
   (c) demonstrate against trade with South Africa?
2 Apartheid also applies to sport.
   (a) Do you think that British cricket and rugby teams should play against South Africa?
   (b) South Africa has been banned from the Olympic movement. Do you think this is right?

(c)  In 1984 Zola Budd, a young white South African record-holder, was given British citizenship in 10 days so that she could run under the British flag in the Los Angeles Olympics. An Asian woman in the East End of London was heard to say, 'I've been waiting for my citizenship for 10 years, but the only thing I've ever run for is a bus.' Do you think that it was right that Zola Budd should have been given British citizenship? How do you think black people in Britain and South Africa feel about it?

## Relations between people of different faiths

Because Britain is a multiracial community it is also a multi-faith country. The relationships between people of different faiths is obviously linked to the question of interracial relationships, since different religions are often concentrated in particular parts of the world.

*Test Your Knowledge*

Here are six photographs. Each one is associated with a different religion. Can you say what these religions are? How much do you know about them?

Estimated figures for membership of religious groups other than Christians in the UK.

| | |
|---|---|
| Muslim | 1 000 000 |
| Jews | 412 000 |
| Hindus | 400 000 |
| Sikhs | 200 000 |
| Buddhists | many thousands |
| Bahai's | many thousands |
| Rastafarians | many thousands |
| Jains | several hundred |
| Zoroastrians | several hundred |

Like Christianity, most of these religions have a number of subdivisions.

For the British in the past, as for most Europeans, Christianity and colonialism went hand in hand. Where the Empire went the missionaries soon followed, taking with them the faith and culture of Europe.

Christianity is a missionary religion – that is, it sees the task of converting other people to the faith as part of its witness. It has been a common belief among Christians that their religion is the only way to salvation, and that it is the religion which contains the full truth about God. However, as people of different faiths have begun to meet together and share their ideas, many of them have become aware of the depths of spirituality in every religion. Many Christians have come to feel that they can learn from, as well as teach, people of other faiths.

---

### Something to discuss and write about
*Where can I find God?* Discuss the following statements.

---

- Some religions claim to have a special revelation from God; but God only revealed himself fully in Jesus Christ and Christianity is the only religion which contains *all* the truth about God. It is the only path to salvation.
- There is one God, and he has shown himself through different people and through different cultures. He has many messengers who have taught people about God in the way they can best understand. No single religion can claim to possess a greater portion of the truth than others.
- Every religion has provided a meaningful way of life for millions of people, and this way of life is usually connected to the culture of particular countries. People should not be expected to change their religion to one which is tied to a culture which is foreign to them.
- If you believe that your religion *does* teach the full truth about God and is the only way to salvation, you have a moral duty to teach it to others.

- Christianity can learn a lot from other religions. It can get a new lease of life by contact with people who hold other points of view, have different practices, and contribute new insights.

## Tough questions for British Christians

Here are some points raised about Christianity by non-Christians (agnostics as well as people who practise non-Christian religions). How do you think a Christian can answer these points?

1 The traditional Churches are becoming stale and too concerned with their own institutions. Fewer people than ever are going to church, while some are being attracted to the Eastern religions such as Buddhism.

2 In schools it is obvious that Muslim, Jewish and Hindu children know far more about their religion than most Christian children do about theirs. This shows that Christian families are no longer teaching their children religious beliefs and values.

3 More than that – Muslim, Jewish, Hindu and Sikh children frequently know more about *Christianity* than do Christian children!

4 British society shows a lack of respect for morality, the elderly, religion, religious leaders, and is generally lacking in spiritual values. The Church seems unable to do anything about this.

5 Christianity does not have a very good record. In the past (and in some places in the present) it has been responsible for such evils as the Crusades, imperialism, *apartheid*, racism and slavery.

6 Christianity in Britain has suffered from being the established religion. It is easy to be a Christian. No one persecutes you for it, and you never have to explain your belief or justify it. Christianity is far more alive in countries like Poland and Russia where it has to face unsympathetic governments, and in countries of the Near and Far East where it exists side by side with other religions, and Christians are constantly having to argue their case.

## Judaism and other faiths

The vast majority of Jews living in Britain today aim to enter as fully as possible into the life of the community while preserving their own traditions, beliefs and culture.

The Jewish communities in Europe have suffered terribly at the hands of their Christian neighbours in the past, and one aim of British Jewry today is to bring the public to a fuller understanding of the Jewish religion and way of life. Nowadays thousands of children every year are welcomed on school visits to their local synagogues, and it is not rare to find the local Rabbi taking morning assembly in school. On a national level, slots like 'Thought for the Day' on Radio 4 are now often done by representatives of religions other than Christianity, and many of the British public have come to know and respect the wit and deep insights of speakers like Rabbi Lionel Blue.

Most Jews and Christians are aware that they share many ideas in common, such as a reverence for the books of the Old Testament (Tenach) and a belief in one God. One Rabbi always explains the similarity to visiting schoolchildren by saying, 'When a Jew and a Christian meet, they each feel that they are seeing themselves as if in one of those fairground twisted mirrors. What each person sees is himself, but the image is distorted.'

It is not uncommon now to find Jews and Christians joining together in common enterprises and sometimes in prayer. Anyone is welcome at most synagogue services regardless of their faith. The Jewish Board of Deputies supports the work of the Council of Christians and Jews, seeing it as a means of fighting religious and racial intolerance.

### Islam and other faiths

As in any religious group, there are Muslims who are not interested in finding common ground with other faiths. But in Britain most Muslims welcome non-Muslims to their mosques, and like the leading Jewish organisations, are interested in producing educational materials so that the teachings of Islam can be better understood. Many Muslims, while remaining strictly faithful to their own belief and tradition, are anxious to learn more about Judaism and Christianity in particular, recognising that all three religions are monotheist. Many Muslim writers are saddened by the divisions between the three great faiths of the West, for they feel that by acting together over matters like poverty and world peace these religions could influence governments far more than if they acted separately.

### Hinduism and other faiths

Hinduism has no difficulty in respecting the teaching of all religions. The Hindu believes that there are many paths to God and that they are all of value. It is not unusual for Hindu children to be taught about Jesus, Mohammed, Moses or Abraham as religious leaders who set us all an example – alongside Rama and Krishna. Indeed, many Hindu children these days seem to know popular Bible stories better than children from Christian families. India, the home of Hinduism, is a truly multi-faith society, encompassing also Islam, Sikhism, Buddhism, Jainism and Christianity in large numbers. For the most part, although not always, these religions have learnt to live side by side in peace. It is not unusual when visiting a Hindu temple in Britain to find a prayer-hall dedicated to all religions, and often also a library with books about all religions. Often, services are held in these prayer-halls which members of all religions are encouraged to attend.

### Dialogue

Dialogue is the word used to describe a meeting or debate between people of different faiths. Many people feel that studying 'world religions' from a textbook is not enough. People of different faiths, and none, must come together to share their views and be prepared to learn from each other.

There are many misunderstandings between religions. Non-Christians often associate Christianity with standards of Western morality and materialism. Christians often think of Muslims as violent. Some Muslims think that Christians believe in three gods. Dialogue for most people involves understanding what others believe while remaining faithful to your own religion.

---

'We need to appreciate what others believe. But it must be with a real understanding, which does not gloss over the differences. When it is a matter of heaven or hell, of salvation, how can we be indifferent? It is no good saying superficially we are all the same – we are not.

'In showing appreciation, there are acts of courtesy that help. For instance, when Muslims are fasting it might be courteous of others not to eat or drink with them for an hour. And Muslims might refrain from serving meat when there are Hindus present.'

Enche Uthman al Muhammadi, Department of
Islamic Studies, University of Malaya

'The different religions are like a tree. There is one root and many branches. On each branch there is a light, and the lights are of differing colours. But they all draw their light from the one root.

'We all need to keep our own light bright.'

Sayyeda Fatima al-Yashrutiyya

---

But there is plenty of common ground (see chapter 6). Most people of faith (excluding a small minority of extremists) have a real desire for peace and justice. They want a better world and are deeply concerned with issues like health, poverty, ecology, and education. Perhaps by working together they can achieve more than if each religion works alone.

## *Working for inter-faith understanding*
### *Sacred Trinity Centre, Salford*

In 1978 Sacred Trinity Church in Salford, Manchester, was handed over to the Christian Education Movement as a centre for 'Religion and Education in the Inner City'. It is now a place where people of all religions can meet and study, and where local problems are discussed.

The idea behind the centre is that people who live together in a community must try to understand each others' customs, and these customs are often based on religious values.

Sacred Trinity has become well-known to children in the Manchester area because of its development of urban trails. The trails are day, or half-day, visits to religious communities in the area. The children go to shops and places of worship, and meet community leaders. The idea of the trails set up at Sacred Trinity has been copied elsewhere in the country.

### The Council of Christians and Jews

Outside the concentration camp at Dachau is a memorial to the Jews who died there in the 1930s and 1940s. On it are written the words NEVER AGAIN.

The atrocities committed by the Nazis showed the full horror of what racism could lead to, and after the war, many European Christians were determined to make anti-Semitism a thing of the past.

The Council of Christians and Jews was set up in 1942 'to check and combat all forms of religious and racial intolerance; to promote mutual understanding and goodwill between Christians and Jews in all sections of the community; to promote fellowship between Christian and Jewish youth organisations in educational and cultural activities; and to foster cooperation between Christians and Jews in social and community service'.

*Answers to the quiz on pages 39–40.*
1 True. In 1982 202 000 people entered the country and 259 000 left. This has been the trend for many years, the only exception being 1979.
2 Ireland. 3 2m. 4 4%. 5 Leicester 21.3% Birmingham 16.3% Bradford 15.7% Wolverhampton 15.4% Greater London 14.3% Manchester 7.8% Bristol 4.0% Liverpool 1.7% Sunderland 0.7%. 6 False. Holland and France especially have many black citizens. 7 False. There was one in the Commons and two in the Lords. 8 Con.2 Lab.2 Lib.4.
9 The TGWU had one. 10 One – appointed in 1985.

# 4 Family and friends

## Making relationships

Have you ever had one of those awful arguments with a friend or a member of the family which has led to a time of complete hostility? You do not talk to each other; you both get into huddles with friends who take your side; there are whispered conversations in corners; dark looks across the room. Most of us have been in this situation, and happily, have usually found a way of sorting out the differences. Yet arguments like these cause us some of the greatest unhappiness in our lives. The break-up of a relationship, if it is not healed, can lead to severe depression or even suicide. The reason for this is that people are very important to us.

---

### *Something to discuss and write about*

1 Why do you think it is that we get on well with some people and not with others? What factors influence your choice of friends?

2 What qualities of friendship would you like to think your friends found in you?

3 What sort of things in your experience:
  (a) cause a breakdown in friendships?
  (b) strengthen friendships?

---

*Getting on with people – what the New Testament says*

> If you love only those who love you, what reward can you expect? Surely even the tax-collectors do that

Parents often say to their children: 'I don't want you going around with him/her.' They say this about certain children because they feel that they are 'bad company', and that they will get other children into trouble. But it was often these very undesirable people – bad company, in fact – that Jesus made friends with. How would your mother feel if you took Mary Magdalene home?

Read the following passages and find out what sort of people Jesus befriended. Can you think of any people in your society who have the same sort of position as these people did?

Matt. 9:9–13; 26:6–13; Mk 1:16–20; 2:17.

On one occasion (Matt. 5:43–5) Jesus said that anyone can like their friends; it is loving people you do *not* like that is difficult. Children are often very cruel to people they do not like, and unfortunately adults are sometimes not much better. People who get 'picked on' are often vulnerable in some way, and people find that winning a victory over them with words or fists gives them a feeling of strength and power.

All religions teach that taking advantage of the weak is wrong. Not only does it cause them to become bitter, but the feeling of satisfaction at causing misery to another can only be regarded as degrading to the aggressor.

---

### Something to discuss

Antony is 14 years old. He is small for his age and also quite immature at a time when most of his classmates at school are beginning to grow up. No one has ever liked Antony, except another boy two years below him who goes around with him. Antony has several annoying habits which irritate other members of his class. He flicks paper at them during lessons, kicks them under the table, grabs their pencil cases and hides them. He does all this very quietly, but his victims tend to shout at him which draws the attention of the teacher to themselves. To make matters worse, when the teacher tells the 'victims' off for shouting and they explain the problem, Antony looks innocent and denies all knowledge of the affair! The other children in the class get their own back by blaming Antony for everything that goes wrong. They call him names and taunt him about his size. He is in fact a very unhappy boy, but no one notices that.

1 Why do you think Antony behaves as he does?
2 Is the behaviour of the other children likely to make Antony better or worse?
3 What might the other children do to help Antony behave in a more reasonable way?

**Love is** . . .

Jesus said, 'Love your enemies'. He obviously did not mean that we should hold strong feelings of affection for people we do not like. These days, love is often seen as meaning the same as 'being in love'. But in fact, most people are probably not 'in love' with most of the things and people they 'love'.

---

**Something to discuss and write about**

The word love is used to describe many emotions. Here are ten people talking about love. In each case discuss:
- (a) What emotions the speaker is experiencing.
- (b) What actions they might take as a result of their love.
- (c) How they would feel if the object of their love was taken away.

1  'I really love this book.'
2  'I love my teddy bear.'
3  'I love my friends.'
4  'I've fallen in love with a girl I met at the party last Saturday.'
5  'I love my husband as much now as I did when I married him twenty years ago.'
6  'I love my dog.'
7  'I love gymnastics.'
8  'I love God.'
9  'I love people.'
10  'I love my parents.'

---

**Research**

Discuss the meaning of 'love' in the following passages:
1  I Corinthians 13
2  John 13:1−7
3  John 15:12−13
4  John 12:28−34

---

'Man cannot live without love'
(Pope John Paul II)

'Loving implies commitment to the other person, involvement in that person's life, whatever it may cost in suffering.'
(A Quaker View of Sex)

---

## Sexuality

One aspect of human existence which has a considerable effect on our relationships is our sexuality. Most people experience a special form of loving relationship which involves sexual attraction, and sometimes sexual contacts. These relationships may be some of the most important in our lives, for they may decide who we choose to live with or marry, and who is to be the father or mother of our children. Before we go on to study these relationships, we should consider briefly what we mean when we talk of people as male and female. Does this mean that we are putting people into two categories with very different characteristics?

---

**Something to discuss and write about**

1 People sometimes talk about 'male' and 'female' characteristics. Do you believe that these characteristics exist (apart from the obvious physical ones)? If so, what do you think they are?

2 Even if you do not attend a mixed school, you probably belong to some sort of group consisting of boys and girls. Have you noticed any differences in the behaviour and emotional development of boys and girls, both as individuals and in groups? If so, what do you think causes these differences?

3 In what ways do you expect your sex to affect your future life – e.g. might it influence your choice of job? What do you expect your role to be in your family if you have one?

4 What problems might there be in a relationship between a boy and a girl which might not be present in close friendship between two people of the same sex?

---

## Religion and sexuality

Most religions in the world have rules relating to 'opposite-sex' relationships. Many religions also have traditions about the role of men and women in the family and in society. It may seem at times that some of the work in this chapter is very sociological; and so it is, simply because so many customs and laws in society derive from religious traditions. In fact, it would not be going too far to say that the family and social structure of most countries has been decided by the religion which has traditionally dominated that country (e.g. in some Muslim countries men are allowed more than one wife).

In the Western world at least, traditional religious teachings are being questioned, not only by the young, and not only by people who are not religious. One Christian report openly states: 'Many professing Christians are themselves no longer certain what are the true implications of Christianity for sexual relationships.' (*A Quaker View of Sex*)

This is also true of people belonging to other religions. Many Muslim and Hindu families living in Britain are alarmed to find their young people rejecting the traditional standards of their faith.

### Christianity and sex

The Church can sometimes give the impression of being obsessed with sexual matters and with marriage. This may seem odd to people who realise that such subjects did not apparently form a major part of the teaching of Jesus or the New Testament in general. Certainly other subjects like the use of wealth and the need for peace and love feature more prominently. But our sexuality is a powerful force. It affects our relationships with one another and has far-reaching social and psychological consequences. The Church knows this, and in recent years, most branches of the Christian Church have held inquiries and produced reports on such matters as sex outside marriage, homosexuality, marriage, family life and second marriages for divorcees, and many others.

*Christian attitudes to sex in the past*
1 Christianity inherited a strict moral code from its parent religion, Judaism, which at the time when the New Testament was written, stressed the need for higher standards of sexual behaviour than many of the surrounding nations had.
2 From about 100 BC to about 300 AD there were a number of popular religions in existence which were collectively known as Gnosticism (see Introduction). These religions taught that material things, including the human body, were evil. Some Christians were influenced by this point of view, and there were some Christians who thought they should work for higher spiritual values over against the 'desires of the flesh'.
3 The powerful monastic movement with its emphasis on celibacy developed early in the Church's history. The idea that celibacy was the mark of 'super-Christians' and marriage only second-best carried considerable weight in some circles, and even today the Greek Orthodox Church has orders of celibate and married priests. Only celibates can become bishops. In the Roman Catholic Church priests are not allowed to marry, although the argument for this today is that they need freedom from the ties of marriage if they are to devote themselves properly to their work. Also in the past virginity has been highly valued among women, most female saints having been virgins.
4 Until the Reformation in the sixteenth century, the Church consisted mostly of married people and their families, but was led by celibate priests and monks. This must surely have had an influence on Christian thinking about sex.

---

**Something to discuss and write about**
Here are some ideas about sexuality that have been put forward by Christian groups.

---

1 God is the creator who made human beings in his own image. Sexuality is a gift from God which enables the created order to continue. Sex itself is not good or evil but neutral.

2 Sex can be used for good or evil.

3 Sexual expression can play an important part in a loving relationship by enriching it.

4 Animals perform sexual acts where and when they please. But we are not animals and there must be some rules which govern our sexual behaviour.

5 It is wrong to exploit another person, to use them simply to gratify our needs and desires.

6 Marriage and the family still form the most stable basis for a smoothly-running society and must be preserved.

### Sex outside marriage

By the age of sixteen, many people have become aware of, or have had experience of a degree of physical contact in some of their relationships, usually with the opposite sex.

Most religions teach that sexual contact should be something reserved for married people. Muslim, Hindu and Sikh girls are often shocked at the degree of freedom allowed to Western girls, since they themselves are often sheltered from unchaperoned contact with boys.

Although Christian teaching still emphasises that a sexual relationship should be reserved for marriage, not all Christians hold this point of view.

> **Something to discuss and write about**
> Here are some points made by people who believe that a sexual relationship should only exist within marriage. How do you think these points might be answered by people who disagree with them?

1 A sexual relationship involves more than 'biology'. It should be a part of a deep and loving relationship between two people who are totally committed to each other.

2 A sexual relationship involves responsibility. The primary purpose of sex is reproduction, and even with the use of contraceptives, the sex act may lead to pregnancy. There should be no possibility of this happening outside marriage.

3 Sometimes a girl might have sex with her boyfriend because she is afraid of losing him. If she allows herself to be blackmailed in this way she will probably regret it later, and realise that she has been used.

4 Sex is something very special. It is a total giving of yourself, and should be reserved only for that person with whom you promise to spend the rest of your life.

> Here are some points raised by people who believe that, in some circumstances at least, there is nothing wrong with having sex with someone to whom you are not married. How might these points be answered by those who do not agree?

1 Sex is a purely physical need, like eating. There is nothing wrong with satisfying this need.

2 Everyone says that teenage marriages have less chance of success. If people are expected to wait at least until their mid-twenties before they marry, it is unreasonable to expect them to wait this long before having a sexual relationship, especially bearing in mind that the sex-drive is at its height for many people in the late teens and early twenties.

3 Many people these days do not agree with marriage but have a permanent relationship with another person without getting married. It is quite reasonable that sex should play an important part in such a relationship.

4 We are given the impression that it is usual for people to have sexual experience in their teens. Anyone who does not is bound to feel left out.

5 Boys are expected to be sexually experienced. Girls like them better that way. Also it has always been accepted that boys should have sexual experience before they are married. Girls however need to be more careful. There is always the risk of pregnancy, and a girl who is sexually experienced may get herself a bad reputation.

## Religion and marriage

Most people who have a religious marriage ceremony in this country will be married in a Christian church. Here are some of the things that are said during the Anglican church service, which can help us understand how many Christians view marriage:

Grant to your servants that, loving one another, they may continue in your love until their lives' end. . . . The Scriptures teach us that marriage is a gift of God in creation and a means of his grace, a holy mystery in which man and woman become one flesh. It is God's purpose that, as husband and wife give themselves to each other in love throughout their lives, they will be united in that love as Christ is united with his Church.

Marriage is given that husband and wife may comfort and help each other, living faithfully together in need, in plenty, in sorrow and joy . . .

. . . the joy of their bodily union may strengthen the union of their hearts.

Marriage is given that they may have children and be blessed in caring for them and bringing them up in accordance with God's will.

Marriage must not be undertaken carelessly, lightly or selfishly, but reverently, responsibly and after serious thought.

In a marriage, husband and wife belong to one another and they begin a new life in the community.

They will join hands and exchange solemn vows and in token of this they will give and receive a ring.

The vows you are about to make are to be made in the name of God . . .

'Tom, will you take Claire to be your wife? Will you love her, comfort her, honour and protect her, and forsaking all others, be faithful to her as long as you both shall live?'

'I, Claire, take you, Tom, to be my husband, to have and to hold from this day forward; for better for worse, for richer for poorer, in sickness and in health, to love and to cherish, till death us do part, according to God's holy law; and this is my solemn vow.'

'I give you this ring as a sign of our marriage. With my body I honour you, all that I am I give you, and all that I have I share with you, within the love of God, Father, Son and Holy Spirit.'

An Anglican report, *Marriage and the Church's Task* (1978), defined marriage in the following way. Do you agree with these definitions?

### Marriage is . . .

1 A *loving* relationship based on mutual affection and shared values.
2 A *sexual* relationship based on mutual attraction and shared physical satisfaction.
3 A *social* relationship which includes both families and a network of contacts.
4 A *biological* relationship leading to the birth and nurture of children.
5 An *economic* relationship based on common property, home, possession and income.

### Marriage and the Catholic Church

The Roman Catholic Church, the Greek Orthodox Church and some Anglicans regard marriage as a sacrament. A sacrament is a sign which is believed to have an actual effect – so for example the bread and wine of the Mass become the body and blood of Christ. Christians who think of marriage as a sacrament believe that when two baptised people marry, God is present, giving his grace, not just on their wedding day but for the rest of their lives. In the sacrament of marriage, God is present, giving to the relationship the gift of grace. Catholic writer Dr Jack Dominian explains this grace in the following way. Both partners in a marriage expect emotional and material support from one another. They expect 'the wounds that they brought into marriage' to be healed by their partner. Within a marriage, one partner often has in emotional and practical terms what the other lacks, and partners in marriage often complement each other. Dr Dominian talks of marriage as a healing relationship: '... marriage, if properly understood, will become the most common source of healing in society' (*An Outline of Contemporary Christian Marriage*). What sort of 'healing' do you think can take place within marriage?

---

**Something to discuss and write about**
Tackle the following issues connected with marriage.

---

1 Why do some people who are not practising Christians get married in Church?
  (a) Do you think this is hypocritical?
  (b) Do you think that clergy should be able to refuse to marry people if they are not convinced that they really do believe in the Christian ideas of marriage?
2 Should everyone who goes through a religious marriage ceremony, where they promise to be faithful to each other for life, go to marriage-preparation classes? If you think so,
  (a) what do you think should be discussed in marriage-preparation classes?
  (b) who should lead the classes? Should it always be the priest?
3 Study the Anglican marriage service.
  (a) What reasons are given for marriage?
  (b) What attitude towards marriage is expected of the couple?
  (c) What vows are made?
4 Do you think that husband and wife should *both* wear a ring?
5 At the wedding of the Prince of Wales, the Archbishop of Canterbury said, 'This is not the end but the beginning.' Do you think that there is a danger of people thinking of marriage as the end of a fairy tale, and not looking forward enough to the realities of married life ahead?
6 Mr Collins to be sure was neither sensible nor agreeable; his society was irksome, and his attachment to her must be imaginary. But still he would be her husband. Without thinking highly either of men or of matrimony, marriage had always been her object; it was the only honourable provision for well-educated young women of small fortune, and however uncertain of giving happiness, must be their pleasantest preservative from want.
  (Jane Austen, *Pride and Prejudice*, concerning Charlotte Lucas)

Do you think that some girls today hold the same ideas about marriage as did Charlotte? Is it still their main object in life?

## Judaism and marriage
In a Christian marriage service the making of vows before God is the

central act. In a Jewish or Muslim marriage this is not so, and in fact no vows as such are made. Instead, in both these religions, a marriage is primarily a contract.

Judaism no longer supports the idea of 'arranged marriages', although the choice of partner for practising Jews may be limited by their desire to marry someone of their own religion. Certainly many Jewish parents still encourage their children to marry a Jew, and many Orthodox parents would not even be happy with their son or daughter marrying a Liberal or Reform Jew. This is not because the family despise other peoples' religious views but because they realise how difficult it is for one partner in a marriage to continue in a certain religion if their partner is not equally committed to it. (This can be said of Christianity too, where marriages between Catholics and Protestants are often frowned upon for the same reason.)

The central act in a Jewish wedding is the agreement to the terms of a contract (Ketubah) and the signing of this contract. Here are some of the words from the contract:

> Do you ... enter into this holy covenant of affection and truth to take (X) to be your wife/husband in the sight of God and Man?
>
> Do you faithfully promise to be a true and devoted husband/wife to her/him?
>
> By this ring you are married to me in holiness according to the law of Moses and of Israel. (Accompanying an exchange of rings, or with *a* ring, to seal the marriage)

The couple may choose from a number of prayers in the prayer book, but here is one of the prayers often used at weddings. It expresses many ideas which are important to the Jewish idea of marriage.

> Lord, who taught men and women to help and serve each other in marriage, and lead each other into happiness, bless this covenant of affection, these promises of truth. Protect and care for the bridegroom and bride as they go through life together. May they be loving companions, secure in their devotion which deepens with the passing years. In their respect and honour for each other may they find their peace, and in their affection and tenderness their happiness. May your presence be in their home and in their hearts.

## Islam and marriage

Muslim families traditionally favour agreed marriages. This does not mean that Muslim teenagers have no choice as to whom they will marry. Parents will use their experience of life and their contacts to find a partner who, they believe, has the right education and social background to suit their child. But if either the boy or girl is not happy with the match, they have the right to refuse.

There are two important stages in a Muslim wedding. The first is called the Nikah: This is a ceremony where the contract is signed. Each party agrees to take the other, and the groom agrees to pay the woman a dowry – the amount will have been agreed beforehand.

The second stage of the marriage is the Rukhsitania which means the 'farewell'. This is the time when the bride and groom begin to live together as husband and wife. Sometimes the Rukhsitania may take place on the same day as the Nikah, but it is common for it to take place later, even as much as one or two years later if one of the partners is away at University or is unable for some other reason to begin married life.

The Qur'an says that a man may have more than one wife, but in Britain this is not possible as it breaks British civil law. One reason for this practice dates back to times when women commonly outnumbered men, who were often killed in battle. Since the only means of support for a woman was a husband, men were allowed more than one wife to avoid women being destitute.

---

### Something to discuss and write about

1 Read again the words of the Jewish marriage contract and the prayer used at a Jewish wedding. What ideas about marriage are expressed in these passages?

2 (a)  Why might parents be good judges of who will make a suitable partner for their child?

   (b)  What reasons are there, if any, to suppose that a young person has a better chance of finding a suitable marriage partner for themselves than if their parents chose for them?

3 What difficulties do you think might be experienced by a married couple who are followers of different religions? How might they handle these problems?

4 If there are people of different religious faiths in your group, ask them to talk about the ideas regarding the purpose and importance of marriage in their religion.

---

*Should she interfere?*

Shoba Patil is a bright 17-year-old girl, studying three A-level subjects in the sixth form. Her family are devout Hindus and at home they have a shrine room to their special family god, Ganesha. Mr and Mrs Patil have arranged for Shoba to marry a young Hindu lawyer, the son of old friends. They hope to announce the marriage in the near future, and want the civil marriage to take place later in the year. The religious ceremony will take place the following year when Shoba has taken her A-levels.

However, Shoba is not at all happy with the idea. She wants to go to university and study to be a doctor. She knows that competition for entry to medical school is very tough and that she may have to take a place at any university in the country. She does not want to be tied by marriage. In any case, she has spent her whole life in England, and wants the freedom over her own life that she sees in her school friends. She has the right to refuse to marry, but her family are very close and very traditional. To make matters worse, she is the only girl in the family, and her three brothers agree with their parents in their choice of a husband for Shoba. Ravi is, they argue, doing very well, and will provide Shoba with a good home.

One day Shoba decides to confide in Mrs Jenkins, her Head of Year at school. She tells Mrs Jenkins that she is afraid to face her father and tell him that she does not want to marry. The only alternative she can think of is to leave home, but she has nowhere to stay. After some discussion, Mrs Jenkins says that Shoba can come and live with her family for a while, and that she will visit her parents and talk to them. The next day, Shoba leaves home early with a few possessions in a bag, and that evening moves into the Jenkins home.

1 What do you think might have happened next?
2 Do you think that Mrs Jenkins was right to interfere?
3 If you were Mrs Jenkins, what do you think you would have done to help Shoba?
4 How do you think Shoba's parents felt about Mrs Jenkins' actions?
5 Do you think that other Asian teenagers brought up in this country may face the same sort of problems as Shoba? What other problems over loyalties may be faced by the children of Asian immigrants?

*A Hindu wedding.*

6 Do you think that Shoba could have solved the problem by some other means than by leaving home?

## Religion and family life

Most religions stress the importance of family life, seeing stable families as the basis of a stable society. The Christian tradition, amongst others, stresses the need for children to be brought up in loving and secure homes, and there is considerable evidence that adults who had unhappy and insecure childhoods have greater difficulty in producing a stable home for their own children.

---

### Something to discuss and write about

What do you think about these issues connected with parents and families?

---

1 'Honour your Father and your Mother'... Any children from Muslim and Hindu families are shocked at the lack of respect shown to adults by Western children. Why do you think many children are brought up to be polite to adults? Do you think that you might bring up your children to respect adults? If so, what form should this respect take – e.g. should a young person give up a seat on the bus for an older person? Should a young person not 'butt in' when an adult is talking?

2 Parents are legally responsible for their children until they are 18. What does this mean?

3 The bringing up of children is still often regarded as a woman's job.
   (a) Why do you think many men now want to be present at their baby's birth?
   (b) 'Women are better equipped than men for bringing up children.' Argue for and against this view.
   (c) What part do you think the father and mother should each play in bringing up their children?
   (d) Why do many people say that women with children under school-age should not go out to work? Explain your opinion on this subject.

4 Why do many parents teach their religious views to their children? It they do not, what sort of values and standards of behaviour should children be taught at home?

5 Some families keep religious customs in the home, e.g. some Christian families say Grace before meals; many Jewish families say Grace and also have a special meal on Friday nights; Hindu families often have daily prayers at the household shrine. In what ways do you think that keeping these customs might help to make the family closer?

*Say or write as much as you can about the people in this picture and what they are doing.*

6 The elderly are especially valued in Eastern families.
  (a) What contribution do you think grandparents make to the family?
  (b) These days, far more people are living to an old age, and most families at some time have a very elderly relative who is unable to care for themself. What do you think are the reasons why:
    (i) some families have the elderly relative to live with them?
    (ii) some families put the elderly relative in a home?
  What do you think you would do under these circumstances?

## Religion and divorce

Married couples today can expect quite a different marriage from that of their parents or certainly their grandparents. One very basic point is that people are now living for much longer than they did at the end of the century, and consequently a life-long marriage involves people in spending many more years together. Also families are now having fewer children, so the woman spends less of her time in pregnancy and child-rearing, leaving her free to work and enjoy her own pastimes. The position of women in society has undergone a radical change, and it is now accepted in many homes that men and women share domestic chores. Added to this are all the pressures of twentieth-century life, which leave their marks on marriages as well as on individuals.

One sign of this has been the growth in the divorce rate. It is estimated that one in three marriages now end in divorce, the majority of divorcees marrying again. Some people say that marriages are in fact no less happy now than they ever were. The growth in the divorce rate, they say, is due to the fact that divorce is now far easier to obtain than in the past and is socially acceptable. Also the changed status of women means that women who once had little option other than to put up with unhappy marriages are now economically independent and can free themselves if they wish to do so. One thing is certain: the Churches are having to come to terms with the changes in society and the changes in marriage. Above all, Christian communities are having to ask what is the position within the community of those believers who, having taken vows to remain together for life, now find that they are unable to keep those vows.

### Christianity and divorce

Christian teaching has in the past dominated British attitudes to divorce. This teaching in its traditional form is based on the teaching of the New Testament.

> **Research**
> What do the following passages say about divorce?
> 1  Mk 10:2–12; Matt. 5:31–2.
> 2  John 7:53–8.
> 3  1 Corinthians 7:10–11.

The following are the views of three Christian denominations today – the Methodists, Catholics and Anglicans.

*The Methodist Church* recognises that some marriages drag on in intolerable unhappiness for the couple and their children, and accepts that it must be possible to bring such marriages to an end. But divorce should not be encouraged or made easy. It should only be a last resort when a marriage has 'broken down beyond the power of restoration'. The Methodist Church teaches that if divorced people want to marry in church, they should first be interviewed by the minister who may make a decision on his or her own or consult a superior authority. No minister should be forced to conduct a marriage service for a divorced person against his or her will.

*The Roman Catholic Church* does not recognise divorce, nor will it allow divorced persons to marry in Church. However, the Catholic Church will sometimes declare a marriage 'null'. This does not mean that a marriage has ended but rather that it was never a true marriage to begin with. Many Christians including some Catholics do not agree with this teaching, saying that it is a way around the divorce laws.

Here are some of the reasons for which a marriage might be annulled.

1 Immaturity – when the couple married so young that they did not understand at the time what marriage and its obligations really meant.

2 If one of the partners got married 'to see if it would work' and was not aware at the time that it could not be dissolved.

3 If one or both partner was forced or frightened into getting married.

4 If one or both was suffering from a nervous disorder or from insanity, which made them unaware of what they were doing.

5 If the husband was impotent, or if for some other reason the marriage was not consummated.

6 If one or both made the vows with no real intention of keeping them.

Obtaining an annullment can take a long time, and can be expensive. In desperation, some Catholics get a civil divorce, hoping for an annullment later. But by doing this they put themselves outside the Church. Certainly without an annullment they cannot marry in Church.

*The Church of England*, like the Methodist Church, regards divorce as a matter for the law courts, and does not deny communion to divorced persons. However, the Church of England is in several minds over the matter of whether divorced persons should be allowed to marry again in church. Since many people are affected by any decision which may be taken on this matter, it is important to know what the arguments are.

---

**Something to discuss and write about**

Here are some of the arguments put forward on both sides. Discuss these arguments and add any of your own.

---

*Arguments against allowing divorcees to marry in church*

1 Jesus said, 'What God has joined together let no man separate'. When two people marry they become 'one flesh'. If they separate and marry someone else they are going against the teaching of Jesus and cannot be said to be Christians.

2 The divorce rate is high because it is so easy to obtain a divorce in court. If the *Church* now says that people who break their vows can make new ones, who is left to hold families together? So much misery is caused by divorce, especially to children, that it should be discouraged and made difficult to obtain.

3 The Church is watering down its teaching to fit in with what people want. The Church should stand for the traditional ideas of morality and not give in to selfish and easy-going attitudes.

4 There are difficulties in every marriage. Christians are supposed to be caring and tolerant and should be able to sort these problems out. They married 'for better or for worse'. It is not for Christians to walk out of a marriage and into another just because the first has not lived up to their expectations.

5 A priest who is asked to marry a person who has already failed in one marriage has no reason to suppose that they will take their vows more seriously in the second.

*Arguments in favour of marriages for divorcees*
1 The Church should be more concerned with human need than with rules and regulations. Jesus taught forgiveness, and never told anyone that they could not have a second chance. The Church should do the same.
2 At present many Church of England clergy *do* marry divorcees while others do not. It is unfair that some people should be allowed Church weddings just because they have a liberal bishop whereas others do not.
3 Society has changed so much since Jesus' day that we must not expect to be able to apply his teaching directly to our own situation. He taught that a man should not be able to divorce his wife simply by giving her a note of divorce. In those days a woman was dependent on her husband for support, and if he divorced her she would be left destitute. This is no longer the case, and women do not need protecting in the same way.
4 If a couple want a church wedding the 'second time round' it is likely that it means a great deal to them, or they would not go to all the fuss. If people wish to take their vows before God, the Church should not stand in their way.
5 The Church of England already offers a service of blessing for second marriages. This is hypocrisy. If the Church says that being divorced and marrying again is wrong, how can it bless the marriage? If the Church says it will give the marriage its blessing, why not have a proper marriage service?
6 Many first marriages are between very young people. If with greater maturity they discover that their relationship has changed so much that they are no longer compatible, how can the Church fail to be sympathetic and give them a second chance?

## Celibacy
*Sister Margaret*
> She didn't look like a nun. Not a trace of black anywhere. A large cross hanging on a chain around her neck was the only sign of what she was. But as she told us later on, it hadn't always been like that . . . .

Before Sister Margaret came to work in our parish, she lived in a convent with a school attached. But four years ago she asked to be allowed to work as an assistant to a parish priest, and so she came to St Matthew's.
Margaret herself writes:

> When I became a nun at the age of 25, I took the traditional vows of poverty, chastity and obedience. I joined the convent by going through what was very like a wedding service – only I became spiritually married to Christ.
>     I've never cared much about possessions, so taking a vow of poverty didn't worry me much. I think I was a little worried about the vow of celibacy. It's like swearing to be faithful to one partner when you get

married – you really mean it at the time, but sometimes things don't work out like that in the future: you don't know who you're going to meet. Physical attraction is a powerful thing. In the end you have to say, 'I'm going to accept this, even though it might be difficult at times.'

What I've always found difficult is the vow of obedience. I'm a fairly strong-willed person, and I like to act by my own decisions. But obedience to your superior is part of convent discipline – I suppose it's good for the humility!

I think that being a nun working with the parish priest puts you in a special position. People are funny about sex. Some of them think that since I've taken a vow of chastity I must be a total innocent and I can't understand anything about sex at all. Of course this isn't so. Just because I've renounced sexual relationships as such, doesn't mean that I don't experience loving, tender, personal relationships. It is very often this side of a relationship that married couples need help with. Other people have a medieval idea that I'm some sort of saint because I've given up the desires and pleasures of the flesh. I don't think of myself as better than other people at all. I've chosen my way of life. It's right for me, but is no 'better' than the vocation others have for marriage and having children.

I think that there is a place in the Church and in society for people like me. That special position I was talking about – when people get to know me they soon discover that I can form a relationship with them without 'getting involved'. How many women who are having difficulties with their marriage, would trust their husbands to be left alone with another woman in the house? But they don't mind when it's me. They aren't suspicious that I'll let him cry on my shoulder, listen to all his problems and then run off with him!

Yes, it's lonely sometimes. But I'm lucky. With my work, I belong to so many families that going home to an empty flat never worries me for long.

---

### Something to discuss and write about

1 Make sure that you understand the meaning of these words:
   *vow   poverty   chastity   obedience*
2 What do you think makes some people enter religious orders?
3 What do you think you would (a) like, (b) dislike about being a nun or a monk?
4 Try to arrange a visit to a religious community or ask one of the community to come and talk to the class.
5 Some religious orders are 'closed' and their members do not work 'in the world' but stay inside the convent or monastery. Do you think that such communities can make a contribution to our society?

---

## The women's movement

Many women feel that in spite of the changes which have taken place in the status of women, they do not play an influential part in decision-making. Here are some of the points made by women who campaign for women's rights.

1 In most societies in the world, women's opportunities to develop as individuals are not equal to men's. Men have more educational

advantages, better career prospects, better pay and consequently more freedom and independence.

2 The world as it is today was made by men. The most influential people in our society, and the most powerful, are politicians, the military, bishops, lawyers, and financiers. Most of these people are men, so it is hardly surprising that major policy decisions favour men.

3 Even where, as in Britain, legislation has produced a degree of equal opportunities, old attitudes persist. Women must fight to be seen as individuals, not just as the wives of men and the mothers of children.

4 Old attitudes are even encouraged in the Christian religion. In the past, women have been seen as seducers (like Eve), and we have inherited the idea from the Old Testament that women can be unclean, such as at the time of a period or after childbirth. Two of the Church's respected leaders of the past, Augustine and Aquinas, believed that only the male represented complete humanity. A woman is an incomplete man.

## Male supremacy

> The superiority of man and thus the subjection of women, is a fundamental phenomenon of human life
>
> (Piper, *The Biblical View of Sex and Marriage*)

Writers like Piper and C.S. Lewis argue that equality only means that every soul is equal in the eyes of God. That does not mean that every human being is, or should be, equal in their earthly life. Some Christian writers see the attempts of women to gain equality as a result of selfishness and pride. Women should follow the example of the Virgin Mary, say some, who accepted her position with humility.

---

### Something to discuss and write about

1 Over the past fifty years in Britain, women have had increasing opportunities in education, they can enter Parliament and rise to high positions, they can be self-supporting, and no longer have to have so many, if any, children. In what ways do you think these changes have affected (a) women, (b) men, (c) the family, (d) society as a whole?

2 Would you like to see any more changes in the position of women? If so, what changes would you like to see?

3 In what areas do you think women still have fewer opportunites than men?

4 Do you know of any boys who are still brought up to think of themselves as the dominant sex? If so, who is responsible for this?

5 In what ways are women encouraged to please men by their appearance? What image of women is pictured in the press and advertising?

6 What are the arguments for and against a woman having the same opportunities as a man for getting any job, and getting equal pay?

---

*continued*

> 7 Discuss these two statements:
>   He's going to be the first in your life now . . . turn as many of his
>   interests as you can into your own interests, and keep showing him in
>   practical ways that you are interested in him
>           (British Medical Association pamphlet *Getting Married*, 1972)
>
>   [In marriage a woman is] trained to lack assertiveness and self-
>   confidence: to echo her husband's views in public and finally accept
>   them as her own.
>                               (Lee Comer, *Wedlocked Women*)

## Feminist theology

Feminist theology has been a fairly recent development in the USA and from there it spread into Europe and Latin America. In its early days it was particularly influenced by Margaret Fell, the wife of Quaker leader George Fox.

Feminist theology challenges traditional Christian thinking particularly in its references to God as 'he' rather then 'she' and as Father rather than Mother. Some women say that they cannot feel at home in a Church where all the ideas about God are centred on a male image and where the leaders are all male.

> **Something to discuss and write about**
>
> 1 Make a list of the characteristics which you think apply to a father and a list of characteristics which fit your idea of a mother. Does your idea of God focus on male or female characteristics or both?
> 2 Some feminist writers say that we should think of God as 'Our Mother' rather than 'Our Father'. Why do you think that some people object to this idea?

### The ordination of women

> I believe that males and females have distinctive gifts and both sets of gifts
> are indispensable for truly human existence. . . . There is something
> uniquely valuable that men and women bring to the ordained ministry
> and it has been distorted and defective so long as women have been
> debarred.
>                               (Desmond Tutu)

> **Something to discuss and write about**
> Let's see what you think about the following.

1 Do you believe that women have 'distinctive gifts'? If so, what do you think these gifts are?
2 What qualities do you think are needed by a good parish priest? Is there any reason why a woman should not possess these qualities?

3 Do you find this picture offensive? Surprising? How would you feel if you were married by a woman, or your baby was baptised by a woman? In the Christian Church, the 'Free Churches', Methodists, Baptists, URC etc., allow women to become ministers. But the Orthodox, Catholic and Anglican Churches do not allow women to become ordained priests.

In liberal and Reform Judaism, women can become Rabbis, and Sikh women can hold all offices in the temples.

The arguments that surround the question of the ordination of women are both emotional and theological. The whole question may seem irrelevant to some Christians who belong to the Free Churches, but in Britain there are millions of Catholics and Anglicans, and the question does affect them. The Church of England is so tied to the state (being the established Church still), that it would take an Act of Parliament to enable women to be ordained to its ministry.

Many women who feel that they have a vocation to the ordained ministry are angry and unhappy at the Church of England's decision not to ordain them. Many people regard the decision as simply sexist – yet another example of men, in a community dominated by men, failing to understand the needs of women. The argument has been going on for years, and it is important to understand the arguments of both sides, even though they are very complicated at times.

---

**Biblical research**

This is a question where the teaching of the Bible, and especially that of Jesus, is seen to be very important. Look up the following passages and discuss what they say about the status of women.

*Women and Jesus*
   Mark 15:40–41
   Luke 8:1–3; 43–8; 10:38–42; 23:55–24:11
   John 4:1–42; 20:10–18.
*Women in the Early Church*
   Acts 1:14; 16:11–15; 18:1–8; 21:9
   Romans 16:1–2
   1 Cor. 1:11; 11:1–16 (cf Genesis 2:21–2; 3:16; 14:33–5)
   Galatians 3:28
   Ephesians 5:21–4
   Philippians 4:1–3
   1 Tim. 2:9–15; 5:2–16
   I Peter 3:7.

## *Can a woman be a Christian priest?*

There is an important difference between Churches who do ordain women and those who do not. The difference is difficult for a non-Christian to grasp.

In certain Protestant churches, all the jobs that their ministers do may also be carried out by lay people – even celebrating the Lord's Supper. But Catholic and Orthodox Churches, including the Church of England, have *priests*, who are set apart to perform tasks which no other person is allowed to do. No one but a priest may celebrate the Mass (Eucharist), and only a bishop can ordain priests. When a priest stands at the altar with the bread in his hands and says 'This is my body', he is taking the place of Jesus who said those words at the Last Supper. The question is, can a woman stand in for Jesus?

> Did the woman say,
> When she held him for the first time in the dark stable,
> After the pain, the bleeding, and the crying,
> 'This is my body, this is my blood'?
> Did the woman say,
> When she held him for the last time on the dark hill top,
> After the pain, the bleeding, and the dying,
> 'This is my body, this is my blood'?
> Well that she said it to him then,
> For dry men
> In brocaded robes
> Ordain that she shall not say it for him now.
>
> (Francis C. Frank, a seventeenth-century Catholic priest)

**Something to discuss and write about**

Here are just some of the arguments used by people who feel strongly on the issue of ordaining women. Discuss these arguments and see if you can add others of your own.

*Arguments against ordaining women*

1 (a) The Vatican Declaration on the ordination of women in 1976 said that there must be a 'physical resemblance' between Christ and his priests.

(b) 'Only the one wearing the masculine uniform can represent the Lord of the Church.' (C.S. Lewis)

These arguments say that priests must be men because Jesus was a man.

2 Jesus appointed twelve men to be his particular disciples, and told them that they were to be the foundation of his Church. They passed their authority on to others who were also men. For 2000 years the Church has ordained only men, and we should not ignore such a long and powerful tradition.

3 It is a universal truth that man is the head of the woman. Jesus and St Paul gave us this truth for all time. They were not simply complying with the social rules of their time. You cannot 'explain away' bits of the New Testament which you do not agree with by saying that 'things have changed now'.

4 Jesus *did* depart from accepted social conventions in some matters. He disagreed with Jewish leaders over the purpose of the Sabbath for example. If he disagreed with the accepted place of women, he would have said so.

5 Some people say that certain women feel that the Spirit has called them to be priests. It is very easy to say that the Spirit has called you to do something when what you mean is that you *want* to do it. But the Spirit inspired the New Testament writers, and they did *not* say that women should play a leading part in the Church.

6 If women were priests, they would distract male worshippers.

*Arguments in favour of ordaining women*

1 Just because Jesus was a man, this does not mean that all priests have to be men. Jesus was Jewish, but not all priests are Jewish!

2 If a man says that God has called him to be a priest, he is given a chance to test his vocation. There is no reason to doubt women who say that they have been called by God.

3 Jesus came to break down barriers of sex, nationality, race and class. Christians are all one in Christ, so why should only one half of the Christian body be regarded as worthy to represent Jesus?

4 By the standards of his day, Jesus' relationship with women was extraordinary. The Samaritan woman is said to have been the first person to whom Jesus revealed himself as the Messiah, and Martha was the first person to have faith without seeing a sign. In Luke chapter 10 Jesus actually says that Mary has chosen the 'better part' by listening to his teaching rather than doing the housework.

5 Jesus raised women to the same position as men, but men used their position in society to gain supremacy in the Church.

6 In the past, society has not allowed women a leading role. But now

things have changed. Women are now capable theologians and teachers. The fact that they are now saying that the Spirit is calling them to be priests shows that the time is right to ordain women.

## The place of women in other faiths
### Islam and the position of women

The position of women in Muslim society varies tremendously from country to country and from family to family. The British popular press has often been accused of presenting Muslim women as oppressed and ill-used. In fact there is little to suggest that Muslim women as a whole are any more oppressed than are women from other faiths. Islam does not stress 'superiority' and 'inferiority' when defining the roles of men and women, but may stress the differences in male and female roles. Muslim women are traditionally important as wives and mothers, but in countries like Britain many Muslim girls are learning to integrate with Western society at work or college without losing their distinctive traditions and cultural values. As with any culture, the role of a Muslim girl or woman in her family will depend a lot on how far the family keeps to the faith and traditional customs and ideas. It may also depend on the country in which she lives.

As a result of the contract signed at marriage, Muslim women have their own property, which, Muslim writers often point out, British women did not have until 1876. Islam may recognise the leadership of men in society but not their domination. The different rights and duties of women are seen as complementary. The woman has real control of domestic affairs, may be required to dress modestly and bring up the children. This is no more or less than was expected of any woman born in Britain until comparatively recent times. What many Muslims are fighting to resist is the situation now often found in Western societies where men and women work, leaving children and the elderly to fend for themselves. However, for economic reasons, a growing number of Muslim women in Britain are being forced to go out to work.

Many Muslims feel that in the West, women are regarded as slaves to their husbands, and that Western women are exploited as sex symbols by men who see them as objects of pleasure. Since Western people often say exactly the same thing about Muslim women, this is clearly an area where greater inter-faith understanding is necessary. One Muslim writer says:

> To have equality . . . would destroy the social balance. Society would not prosper but instead would have insoluble problems such as broken marriages, illegitimate children and the break-up of family life. These problems are already rife in Western society. Schoolgirl pregnancies, an increase in abortions, divorce and many other problems have cropped up because of the permissive outlook and so called freedom of women.
> (G. Sarwar, *Islam Beliefs and Teachings*, Muslim Educational Trust)

Another point is worth noticing with respect to the position of women in Islam. Islam, like Christianity, is a world-wide religion, and it has spread to many countries with different cultures. We sometimes hear stories reported in the press about the repression of Muslim women. The repression of women in these cases is not because they are Muslim. It goes back to native customs in that particular country and is not representative of Islam as a whole. In fact Mohammed himself did a lot to safeguard the rights of women, but many of these rights have been taken away, not by the teaching of Islam, but by later changes in the social and political structure of some Muslim countries.

*Hinduism and the position of women*
As with Islam, it is traditionally accepted that the Hindu woman runs the home. The position of women in Hinduism has changed since the days when they threw themselves on their husbands' funeral pyres. The modern Hindu woman in Britain often works for a living and in many families it is the woman who is in charge of family finances. In India women play an important part in politics, and one of India's most famous leaders in recent times was Indira Gandhi, the prime minister who was assassinated in 1984.

The female identity is important in Hindu religion where there are both male and female gods.

*Judaism and the position of women*
Most Jewish women in Europe and America are completely Wester-
nised socially, although – within orthodox Judaism especially – there
are still different roles for men and women. For example, in Orthodox
synagogues men and women sit apart, and at strict Orthodox youth
clubs, boys and girls do not dance together. However, in Liberal and
Reform Judaism women play an equal part in worship and can
become rabbis.

It must be emphasised that as with most issues, it is not possible to
say that there is *one* attitude towards women in any religious
tradition. In most religions the orthodox and conservative branches
will understandably be stricter in their attitude to traditional roles and
values while the liberal branches will be more willing to adapt to
changing social positions.

## Homosexuality

*What is homosexuality?*
A homosexual is a person, male or female, who is physically and
emotionally attracted to people of the same sex as themselves. This is
not the same as the strong sentimental attraction which often exists
between people of the same sex. The 'schoolgirl crush' for example is
a generally experienced phenomenon which usually passes. The fact
that a 13-year-old girl idolises a female teacher, or that a 13-year-old
boy worships the very ground his favourite football star walks on,
does not mean that they are homosexual.

Also it is important to realise that to call someone 'homosexual',
'lesbian' or 'gay', is to describe only one aspect of their personalities.
Many people are colour-blind, but we do not label them as 'colour-
blind' as though that were the only thing worth saying about them.

No one really knows why some people are homosexual. Some say
that there are genetic causes, so that it is with you from birth, others
say that it is environmental (the effect of upbringing). Other theories
suggest that it has something to do with the relationship between
mother and child in the early years. Very few people choose to be
homosexual – it is something that they are. The famous document *A
Quaker View of Sex* compared homosexuality with left-handedness. It
is neither a disease to be cured nor a moral disorder to be condemned.

*Emotional pressures*
It is not always easy for a homosexual couple to maintain a lasting
relationship. This is partly due to the attitude of society which can at
times be unsympathetic. It is often more difficult for a such a couple
to share the joy of their relationship with friends and relatives than it
is for a heterosexual couple, whose relationship will not be frowned

on. There are other problems to be faced as well, some of them purely practical. For example, if one partner is taken to hospital, the other may not be given the authority of next of kin. If one dies, the other may not be given time off work which would be granted to a husband or wife.

## Christianity and homosexuality

In 1967 the Sexual Offences Act was passed in Parliament. As a result, action could no longer be taken against men who performed homosexual acts in private. (Interestingly the law has always ignored lesbianism.) It was now more possible for homosexuals to 'come out' and declare themselves. Over the years it became apparent that no small number were Christians, and some were clergymen. The Churches could not ignore this fact, and over the last twenty years most of the Churches have issued documents stating their view on the subject. Needless to say, there is no one Christian attitude towards homosexuality.

The Churches were generally agreed that no one could be blamed for being homosexual. The two important questions were these:

(a) Should Christians condemn sexual acts between homosexuals?
(b) What should be the Church's attitude towards homosexuals as people?

The Methodist report was sympathetic, saying that the same considerations should be applied to 'gay' relationships as to hetero-sexual ones. In other words the relationship should be judged by its loving nature and stability. However, not all Methodist congregations accepted the report because some felt that homosexual behaviour was unacceptable for a Christian.

The Church of England has issued a number of statements. In one (*Homosexual Relationships*) it states:

> There are circumstances in which individuals may justifiably choose to enter into a homosexual relationship with the hope of enjoying companionship and a physical expression of love similar to that found in marriage.

The Quaker document comes to a similar conclusion, being perhaps the most outspoken in favour of homosexual relationships.

The Roman Catholic Church officially condemns homosexual rela-tionships, although some Roman Catholic writers have tried to ease the situation by saying that homosexuals who cannot control their sex drive are suffering from diminished responsibility and therefore are not really guilty. It must be said that most homosexuals would be highly offended at such a suggestion. Many Roman Catholic writers, however, continue to take the view that although homosexuals cannot help their sexual preference, they should live a celibate life.

## *The Bible and homosexuality*

There is only one passage in the Old Testament which refers without doubt to homosexual relationships, and that is Leviticus 18:22 to 20:13. In the New Testament, St Paul condemns homosexual behaviour in two passages, Romans 1:26–7 and 1 Corinthians 6:9–11. Some people feel that this is all the evidence they need to condemn homosexuality. Others, however, say that these judgements were made long ago when homosexuality was not understood, and at a time when men and women had a social duty to produce children. They would argue that if you take the point of view 'If the Bible says it's wrong, then it's wrong', then you must apply this to *everything* in the Bible. Saint Paul also said that women should keep their heads covered and be silent in church, but many Christians do not take that seriously any more. As for the Old Testament, if we obeyed all its rules, we would still be offering animal sacrifices.

So, yet again, Christians hold very different views. Certainly few Christian homosexuals regard their relationships as incompatible with their Christianity, and there is now a strong 'Gay Christian Movement'. In the end, people's attitudes are likely to be determined by what they see as the primary function of sex: to bring children into the world, or as a contributing factor to a loving relationship.

## *Pastoral care*

Christian teaching is at least fairly unanimous in its assertion that discrimination against homosexuals is wrong. It is argued that the Church should offer a loving welcome to everyone.

The Roman Catholic Church shows great sympathy towards the loneliness experienced by many homosexuals, especially those who have decided to be celibate. Other groups, such as the Quakers, emphasise how important it is that heterosexuals recognise and support homosexual relationships, even if they do not approve of those relationships.

The whole subject is a sensitive one, yet one which involves many people. (It is estimated that there may be three million homosexuals in Britain alone.) It is a subject which raises many questions, to which there are no agreed answers, but it is primarily concerned with people, their security, their welfare and their happiness.

# 5 Matters of life and death

Four doctors are having lunch together in the hospital canteen. One has just performed an abortion on a 15-year-old girl; another is in the middle of an experiment using human embryos; another is a member of a team which specialises in fertilising human eggs in a glass dish; and the fourth knows that after lunch she will have to face the family of a 40-year-old man critically injured in a road accident and tell them that in her opinion his life-support machine should be switched off.

All things considered, it is hardly surprising that many people are complaining that men and women are 'playing God'; we are deciding who shall live, and who shall die; what sex our children will be and when they shall be born. Doctors can now bring life into the world where once it seemed impossible, and can prevent life from beginning where once it would have been inevitable. Death cannot be prevented but it can be delayed, often by several years, and there are people who would like doctors to bring about death in a patient who might otherwise live for years.

These recent developments in medicine affect us all, for we are all likely to be faced with a medical 'moral dilemma' at some time in our lives, even if it is only about whether to use contraceptives, and if so, what sort. 'Medical ethics' is not just something which concerns doctors: it concerns us all.

## Is life sacred?

Many religious people say that life is *sacred*. Sacred means the same as 'holy' – that is, consecrated and set apart as being very special to God. It is said that something 'holy' or 'sacred' must be protected and respected.

Many doctors still take this oath when they join the medical profession:

> The health of my patient will be my first consideration . . .
> I will maintain the utmost respect for human life from the time of conception; even under threat, I will not use my medical knowledge contrary to the laws of humanity.

Jewish, Christian and Muslim tradition states that man was made 'in the image of God' (see chapter 1). This makes human life more important than that of any other species.

> **Something to discuss and write about**
> There are many forms of life in the world, and most of us do not consider it wrong to take the lives of animals for food or clothing. Some people even take the lives of animals for sport. Yet we say that killing humans is wrong. What, if anything, makes human lives more valuable than other forms of life?

While you are studying this chapter, you will need to bear in mind some questions dealt with in other parts of this book, such as the rights of women, wealth, and the problems of world development.

## Religion and contraceptives

> **Research**
> 1 Find out about the various forms of contraceptives available. If you have not learnt about them in another lesson you can get leaflets from your local surgery, or arrange for a speaker from the local Family Planning Clinic to come to your school.
> 2 What difference do you think the availability of contraceptives has had on the family?
> 3 Why do many people think that the use of contraceptives is a good idea?

### *Christianity and contraception*
The official teaching of the Roman Catholic Church is that there should be no sexual act which does not allow for the possibility of pregnancy. The only form of birth control allowed to Roman Catholics is the rhythm method. This means that the couple do not have intercourse on days when the egg is most likely to be fertilised. This teaching was set out in the encyclical *Humanae Vitae*. This document suggests that the use of artificial contraceptives would lead to infidelity within marriage, and would put temptation in the way of the young – especially young men. It also says that a man who is in the habit of using contraceptives 'may forget the reverence due to a woman' and regard her merely as an object to satisfy his desires.

However, it must be said that very many Roman Catholics do not agree with the teaching of their Church on this matter and do in fact disregard it.

Most non-Catholics do not object to using artificial methods of family planning.

But there are particular objections to certain types of contraceptives. These are especially the 'morning-after pill' and the coil which technically cause the abortion of a fertilised egg.

## *Other religions and contraception*

Most Muslim, Hindu and Buddhist leaders allow the use of contraceptives, and most Asian countries have family planning clinics funded by the government. Family planning is less accepted in very poor areas where there is a high rate of infant mortality, but some countries, notably India and China, offer real incentives for couples to have fewer children. In China the financial advantages in having only one child are considerable.

---

**Something to discuss and write about**

1 In September 1984 Pope John Paul II said that even using the rhythm method was wrong if there was no good reason for not having a child. He said that it was wrong to avoid having a child just because you wanted a high standard of living.

Give your arguments for and against this point of view.

2 Why do many people feel that it is important to introduce family planning in Third World countries?

3 Some people say that families in richer countries also have a responsibility to have fewer children because the world is becoming over-populated. What is your opinion on this idea?

---

## *The law and contraception*

In 1984 an English court ruled that doctors should not prescribe contraceptives for girls under the age of 16 without the consent of their parents. The case was taken to the appeal courts and the ruling was overturned by the law lords. The law also states that a man can be taken to court for having sex with a girl under 16, and similarly a woman having sex with a boy under 16 can be charged with indecent assault.

## *A situation to discuss*

Claire is 14. She has been going out with 17-year-old Tony for six months. They have had intercourse on a number of occasions, and Claire is very worried about becoming pregnant. At last she plucks up courage and goes to see her doctor. Doctor Stewart is a strict Protestant, and she does not believe that unmarried people should have sex. She also believes that Claire is too young to be having a sexual relationship. She tells Claire to come back with her mother. But Claire has not told her parents about the full extent of her relationship with Tony, and is afraid to do so now. Doctor Stewart refuses to prescribe contraceptives for Claire, first because the girl is under age, secondly because she will not prescribe without parental consent, and thirdly because she will not assist Claire in committing what she regards as a sin.

1 If you were Claire, what would you do next?

2 Look carefully at the reasons Dr Stewart gave for not prescribing contraceptives. Do you think that they were good reasons?

3 Was Claire right not to tell her parents about her relationship?

4 What do you think about the decision in the original court case that doctors should not prescribe contraceptives without parents' knowledge? Why do you think that the appeal judges changed the decision?

5 It is illegal for anyone to have sex with someone under the age of 16. What arguments could be put, in favour of, and against, this law?

6 Why do some people say that girls under 16 would be less likely to have sex if they could not obtain contraceptives without their parents' consent?

7 Should the doctor's personal views or religion affect her treatment of patients?

## Religion and abortion

The question of abortion brings out very strong emotions in people. We often see demonstrators marching through the streets demanding that abortion be made easier to obtain – and others who are demonstrating for abortion to be made illegal.

An abortion takes place when a doctor removes a foetus from the womb before it has gone the full term of nine months. The result is that the foetus dies. Abortion has been carried out for at least 3000 years, but until 1967 it was illegal in Britain. That is not to say that abortions did not take place (they did – in back streets and usually at the hands of unqualified people, and often with terrible consequences for the women concerned).

## Abortion and the law

The 1967 Abortion Act made four important points.

1 Three doctors must agree before an abortion can take place.
2 No one can be forced to take part in an abortion against her or his will if she or he has conscientious objections.
3 Abortion may only be carried out if:
   (a) There is a risk to the life of the mother, to her physical or mental health, or that of any existing children.
   (b) There is a substantial risk of physical or mental abnormality in the child.
4 An abortion should not take place when the child is capable of being born alive. This has been taken to mean that abortions may not be performed after 28 weeks of pregnancy.

## Some Christian attitudes towards abortion

The Roman Catholic view is that to bring about the death of the mother or the child is 'against the voice of nature and the commandment of God'. Abortion breaks the commandment 'Thou shalt not kill'. The life of the child is as sacred as that of the mother. (This is the view taken in the Papal Encyclical *Casti Conubii*, 1930.)

The Church of England view is given in *Abortion – an ethical decision*. This document says that abortion may be permitted when:

(a) There is a grave risk to the mother.
(b) There is a grave risk that the child will suffer handicap.
(c) After rape.

The Methodist Conference of 1976 agreed with the points made by the Church of England but added that it was important to consider the home background into which the child might be born.

## Judaism and abortion

There is as little agreement in the Jewish world over matters such as abortion as within Christianity, and the arguments used by both sides are very much the same. Many Orthodox Jews are afraid that there is so little respect for human life these days that we should be very careful when deciding in matters of life and death. The Talmud does discuss the question of when life begins. Some arguments state that the foetus is a part of the mother's body, and has no identity because it depends on her for life. Other suggestions include the idea that the foetus does not become a living thing until the head is born. A small minority of rabbis argue that before 40 days of pregnancy the foetus has no status at all, and that abortion may be allowed on any grounds, but many others say that the foetus is at least a 'partial' person. Most rabbis allow abortion where the life of the mother is at risk, though some allow it only in cases of incest or rape. Attitudes among Liberal and Reform Jews are often more relaxed and some even say that since a couple should have no more children than they can afford to clothe and feed, abortion may be allowed on financial grounds. Some also point to conditions of overcrowding and poverty in the world at large and say that women should be free to decide if they want to bring children into an already overcrowded world.

## Islam and abortion

Most Muslim writers agree that contraception is permissible under Islamic law but that sterilisation is not. The arguments are that a woman may be made weak by having too many children, and that families with many children may be reduced to poverty.

Many Muslim writers are also in favour of abortion, and the arguments used are basically the same as those we have already seen used by Jewish, Christian and other writers. But one group of Muslim doctors did a survey because they wanted to test the argument that some foetuses should be aborted because they would come into the world as unwanted children. They did their survey among a group of women who said that they did not want their babies. In no case was the child unwanted after it had been born.

## Two opposing groups
### The Abortion Law Reform Group

This organisation does not think that the present law goes far enough. Its members say that the only person who has the right to decide whether a pregnancy should be terminated is the pregnant woman herself. She should have complete control over what happens to her body, and should decide what is right in her own case without the advice of doctors or anyone else, unless she wants advice.

### The Society For the Protection of the Unborn Child

Just as the previous group put the rights of the mother first, so this group emphasise the rights of the unborn child. Members of this group believe that abortion destroys a human life; in fact it is nothing short of murder.

## When does life begin?

An embryo is unique, for no other will have exactly the same genetic make up. If it goes on growing in the uterus for nine months, the result will be a unique human being. Some people believe that life begins at the moment of conception, and that an embryo can be thought of as having the same rights as a human being. They say that killing an embryo is murder, just like taking the life of a person.

Other people say that since 30–50% of fertilised eggs abort naturally anyway, they cannot be regarded as people. Would it be part of God's plan to lose up to 50% of the 'people' conceived?

At ten weeks the foetus has no developed nervous system and its tiny brain is very different from that of a newborn child. Can this foetus be called a person? Has it a right to live? In traditional Catholic teaching (not held by many these days), the foetus gained its soul at the time when the mother first felt it move. This time was called 'quickening'. Do you believe that we have souls? If so, what is the soul? Where does it come from?

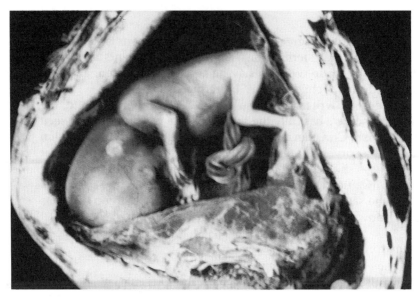

*The foetus at ten weeks.*

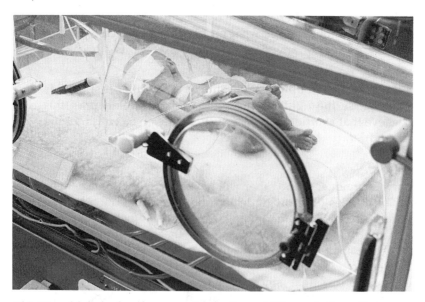

*This 23-week baby has been born prematurely. Every skill known to the medical profession will be used in what will probably be a successful attempt to save it. However, under the present law, this baby may be aborted. If, as does occasionally happen, a live baby is born as the result of an abortion, no attempt may be made to save its life.*

### Something to discuss and write about

1 Look at the case above.
   (a) Does the premature baby have a right to live? Give reasons for your answer.
   (b) Would a foetus of the same age have a right to live (if it was aborted alive)? If not, why not? Give reasons for your answer.

2 A teenage girl is pregnant. But the father of her child is not the man to whom she is engaged. They are both Orthodox Jews and their families are very strict about moral behaviour. She is desperately worried that her parents will throw her out, and that her fiancé will disown her. Many people today would say that she was entitled to an abortion on the grounds of the emotional stress she would suffer. Had this been two thousand years ago, the child in her womb could have been Jesus. Many people say that abortion is wrong because the child in the womb is a potential human being – that is, it is 'destined' to become someone, and if it is aborted, its life, which may have been of supreme importance, would be prevented. Discuss your attitudes to this argument with members of your group.

3 Here is a very difficult question. Many people say that the foetus has no *right* to live because it is not an independent being – it is only part of the mother and cannot exist on its own without her. This gives *her* the right to say whether it lives or dies. But, if you take this view, must you also say that since a young baby also is unable to support itself independently of its mother, it also has no right to live? (We shall come back to this point when we consider the question of euthanasia.)

4 Think of people you know who are under the age of 10 or so. Would you say that they all had a 'right to live'? Working backwards to the time of birth, do you think that there is a time when you can say that a person acquires this right – does it exist from the moment that the cord is cut at birth – or does it exist before that? Could you trace your own life back to the point of conception and say that there was a time when you 'became a person', or do you think that it is in the end impossible to pinpoint such a time? What effect do your answers to these questions have on your attitude to the question of abortion?

5 Do you think that abortion should be encouraged under the following circumstances? Make sure that you can give reasons for your opinion and that you understand the arguments of people who disagree with you.
   (a) Tests proved that a baby was likely to be born mentally handicapped.
   (b) Tests proved that the baby was likely to be born physically handicapped.
   (c) The 'mother' was unmarried and very upset at being pregnant.
   (d) The parents were very poor and already had several other children.
   (e) The 'mother' was unlikely to survive a pregnancy and childbirth.
   (f) The parents already have a grown-up family and the new pregnancy was unexpected and unwanted.
   (g) Tests show that the baby is a girl and the parents wanted a boy. (Private abortions have been known to be carried out for this reason.)

## Abortion – some teenage views

**Tom**. 'What gets me are the women's lib people. They carry on about the right of the woman to decide the fate of the child. But what about the man? If I get a girl pregnant (heaven forbid), that child will be mine as well as hers. Don't I get a say in what happens to it?'

**Maggie**. 'You can argue about abortion until you're blue in the face – what's right and what's wrong: what's moral and what isn't. But when the chips are down and you're pregnant, I reckon that all you want to do is to get rid of it. You aren't going to sit around philosophising about what's the right thing to do.'

**Alan**. 'I think that's a disgusting attitude. If a girl gets pregnant, it's tough on her I admit. But it's a risk she takes, isn't it? If you reckon you're old enough to have sex, then you're old enough to face the consequences and responsibilities. Having an abortion is taking it out on the kid for your mistake.'

**Sharma**. 'What seems to be wrong is the attitude of society. If a girl has a baby well, a white girl at least, there is a long waiting list of people wanting to adopt her baby. So why have an abortion? The only thing I can think of is that girls, and perhaps their parents, are afraid of what the neighbours might say. If no one condemned girls for getting pregnant, I wonder if there'd be so many abortions?'

**Sandra**. 'I agree with that. Also isn't it true that when you become pregnant your body chemicals start adapting you to being pregnant? If you have an abortion it mucks up your hormones and you can end up feeling worse than if you'd gone through with having the baby.'

**John**. 'I know a girl who's had three abortions. She's only 19. I think that's criminal. She's using abortion as a contraceptive.'

**Cheralyne**. 'Isn't it interesting how many boys think abortion is wrong? You aren't the ones who have to go through it all. I agree with Maggie. If I got pregnant I'm blowed if I'd go though nine months of misery as a punishment for a few moments of pleasure.'

## Carol's story

*This is a true story, written by the woman to whom these events happened.*

'Eleven years ago, at the age of 19, I went to Switzerland for a holiday with my mother. While I was there I was raped. It was without doubt the worst moment of my life. It's something I just don't like talking about, and I didn't tell anyone for a year in spite of what happened later.

'But there was more to come. I returned to England and went back to college. I studied, went to parties and generally led the fun life of a student. I kept the memories of my ordeal to myself.

'I missed two periods, but stupidly thought nothing of it. It hadn't occurred to me that I was pregnant until I missed the third period. Then I had a pregnancy test done.

'I'll never forget the day I got the letter saying "positive". I stood on the bridge overlooking the motorway and for the first and only time in my life felt suicidal. The only thing that kept me from killing myself was the fact that I'd also be killing an unborn child. The college doctor made arrangements for me to see a gynaecologist. I was shocked when he told me that he'd already arranged for me to have an abortion. Although I felt generally confused about my future, one thing I knew for certain. I would never have an abortion.

'The next step was one of the worst of my life – telling my mother. I'd been brought up very strictly, and was convinced that she'd disown me. How wrong I was! I can still hear her words: "I'll give you all the strength I have".

'In the months that followed I needed that strength.

'As the fact that I was pregnant gradually sank in, I did a lot of thinking and talking to friends. I was determined to keep the child, however difficult it might be.

'Then I had a talk to a fellow student which really made me stop and think. John was a "mature student". I'd been friends with him for ages and had met his wife and two children on a number of occasions. When I told John about wanting to keep the child he said, "You're either a saint or an idiot". I knew I was neither! He went on to tell me about adoption. I didn't know anything about it, but my first reaction was that it must be tough on the child. "Why?" asked John. "Adopted children are just as much loved as any other child." He then told me that his two children had been adopted. I would never have guessed that they were anything other than his own flesh and blood.

'In the weeks that followed I left college and went to live at home where my "bump" continued to grow. During this time I was constantly thinking about what to do. I realised that my desire to keep the child was selfish. How could I, with no husband and little money, give a baby a good life? All I could offer was love; but love doesn't feed and clothe children. I finally decided to have the baby adopted.

'My mother and I spent hours reading the files the agency gave us on couples wishing to adopt. We chose one. Although I was given the chance of seeing the couple, that was one thing I couldn't face, but my mother, supportive to the last, went to meet them, and her glowing account of them completely reassured me.

'I gave birth to a beautiful 9 lb baby girl. For eight days in hospital I gave her all the love of a lifetime and then said goodbye.

'Of course it was hard; but not for one moment have I regretted the decision. She's 10 years old now, and getting a much better upbringing than I could ever have given her.

'I have always been very open about what happened to me. It is a source of pride for me that I brought another human being into the world, and that I made two people very happy by giving them a child to bring up. I believe in fate: I believe that my child was *meant* to be born, however distressing was the manner of procreation. I have no regrets.'

## 'Test-tube' babies

So far, we have been looking at ways in which life is prevented. But these days just as many doctors are engaged in research to find ways of giving children to people who cannot have any. It is thought that 10%–15% of marriages are childless. Some couples do not want to have children, but more often childlessness is a result of some biological or chemical fault. The most common of all is infertility in the husband. This means that his semen does not carry fertile sperm. Sometimes a woman may not produce eggs, or she may have blocked fallopian tubes.

Some couples accept their inability to have children and remain childless or try to adopt. But others are desperate to have children of their own, and in response to their cries for help, doctors and scientists have developed a number of methods by which childless couples can become parents. The problem is that serious ethical questions have been raised about all of these methods.

It may seem that over the next few pages we lose sight of religious teaching. This is not so. Obviously neither the Bible nor the sacred texts of any other religion says anything about the subjects that are to follow, for we are entering the world of very recent (and in some cases future) scientific discovery. However, for people of all religious beliefs, the important point to consider in all these cases is 'what is life?'. Most of these questions revolve around the question of when life begins, and whether or not life is 'sacred'. A great deal will depend on whether you believe that as soon as a human egg is fertilised, it becomes a vehicle for a living soul.

### Artificial insemination

There are two types of artificial insemination: AIH is artificial insemination by husband, and AID is artificial insemination by donor. These methods have been used since the early 1970s and it is estimated that by the early 1980s about 3000 births had resulted from AID and AIH.

What happens is this. In the case of AIH the husband's sperm is placed in his wife's cervix at the most fertile time of her cycle. It is now common for the couple to perform this 'operation' themselves rather than have it done by a doctor. There are all sorts of reasons for AIH: for example, if a man has a vasectomy he can first have some of his sperm frozen in case he and his wife change their minds, or in case his wife dies and he later wants children from a second marriage.

AID is carried out if the husband is infertile or if he carries a faulty gene which is likely to produce a handicapped child. In these cases the sperm of an anonymous donor is used. Doctors try to find donors of a similar 'type' to the husband, with the same hair, eye and skin colouring. At the moment, the law states that a child born as a result of AID is illegitimate, although it is common practice to put the name of the mother's husband on the birth certificate.

There is a slight risk that in future years children who unknowingly have the same father may have children together. To try to prevent this, it is unusual for one donor to father more than twenty-five children, and it is usual for all those children to be born in different geographical areas.

---

**Something to discuss and write about**

1 The Roman Catholic Church condemns AID. Why do you think this is?
2 What effect do you think it might have on a man to know that 'his' child is not in fact his own biologically, but was the result of AID?
3 As a result of AID there are now many 'sperm banks' to which anyone can apply. This raises some controversial questions. Discuss these questions, noting the arguments of people in your group to disagree.
   (a) Should lesbians be allowed to have children by AID?
   (b) Should single women be allowed to have children by AID?
   (c) Should a woman be allowed to receive the sperm of her dead husband?
   (d) Is AID adultery?
   (e) Is it reasonable for the law to call AID children illegitimate? What could be the legal and economic consequences of this law for an AID child?
   (f) Should a child be told if it was born as a result of AID?
   (g) If a married woman has AID, should her husband be made to sign a paper agreeing to adopt the child as his own before it is born? Might there be any circumstances in which a husband would refuse to accept an AID child after it was born?
   (h) What makes a father? Genes or upbringing?
   (i) An AID child has grandparents and other relatives of which he or she knows nothing. Should they be made aware of the child's existence?
   (j) Should the child have the right to trace his or her biological father in later life?

---

## In-vitro fertilisation

'In vitro' means 'in glass'. In-vitro fertilisation results in what are popularly (and incorrectly!) known as 'test-tube babies'.

There are some cases where AID and AIH will not work – usually because the woman's fallopian tubes are blocked. In these cases the egg and sperm from the parents are fertilised in a glass dish (not a test tube), and once the resulting embryo has divided to the eight-cell stage, it is implanted into the uterus.

## Ethical problems with IVF

For the couple concerned, their only real concern is likely to be that they have a baby. But other people may feel that the side-effects of

IVF are a high price to pay for the happiness of two people.

If IVF is to succeed, drugs are used which make the woman produce two or three eggs at a time – rather than the usual one. The reasons for this are:

(a) First and second attempts to implant embryos usually fail and at least three embryos may be needed.

(b) The process of removing eggs is costly and is a strain on the woman. Doctors prefer to take all the eggs they need at one session.

Sometimes all the embryos are transplanted and this can give rise to three or four babies being born. But often two embryos are implanted and two more left 'on ice' for future use.

Many doctors see great advantages in IVF over natural procreation. They are able to determine the sex of the child from the embryo. This, they argue, could be very important in cases where there is known to be a risk to a child of a certain sex. An obvious example of this is haemophilia which is passed on through the mother but affects mainly boys. If IVF were used with mothers known to be carriers, male embryos would simply not be implanted. Doctors also hope that they may soon be able to remove from male embryos the chemicals which cause haemophilia and other illnesses and replace them with sound chemicals. It is also possible to discover other handicaps by studying embryos after a few days. If it is clear that the baby will be handicapped, the embryo will not be used.

This means that there will be some embryos which are never implanted and which never result in a baby. What do we do with 'unused' embryos? This is the question which bothers a lot of people. We are back to the question, 'when does life begin?' For some, an embryo is a collection of cells: to others it is the beginning of a human life.

## Embryo technology

In fact, human embryos are now used in medical research. This means that after they have been tested by scientists and doctors trying to find out certain information, they are destroyed. There are rules about embryo research:

(a) No embryo used for research may be implanted in a uterus.

(b) The research must be important, e.g. it may shed light on the causes of infertility.

(c) Embryo research may only be carried out with the consent of the 'parents'.

---

### Something to discuss and write about

Here are some tests which are at present carried out on human embryos. Give your reasons for and against these tests being made. You should think carefully about the religious and moral arguments.

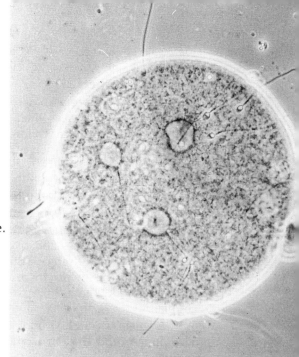

1   This is a picture of a human egg fertilised by a hamster's sperm. The experiment was carried out to provide information about the strength of the walls of the sperm of an infertile man. This might help explain why some sperm cannot penetrate the wall of an egg. This embryo is not allowed to survive beyond the four-cell stage.

2   An embryo is divided into two at the 4–8 cell stage to produce identical twins. One of the new embryos will be tested for abnormalities. If all is well, the other will be implanted into the uterus, and the one used for experiment will be destroyed.

*Fact or science fiction?*

Embryo research is still in its early stages. In the future it may be possible to use embryos in many other ways. Which of the following practices (if any) do you think should be permitted?

1 Embryos can be used in experiments to find out why many miscarriages happen.

2 Embryos will probably be used to find out more about the transmission of disease.

3 Drugs may be tested on human embryos rather than on animals. Some people say that if thalidomide had been tested on human embryos instead of animals, disaster might have been avoided.

4 Should we eventually make *all* births the result of IVF? Doctors could divide all cells at the 4–8 cell stage, implant one embryo and save the other. If, at a later stage, the person who results needs replacement organs, like a heart or liver, it will be possible to grow a new one from tissue taken from the 'spare' embryo. There will be little danger of the body rejecting the new organ because it will have grown from identical tissue.

5 One day it will probably be possible to bring an embryo/foetus to term outside the womb, i.e. we may have 'laboratory-grown' babies.

6 It may be possible one day to take the 'hamster' experiment further and produce cross species of human and animal.

7 It may be possible to bring a human foetus to term in the womb of an animal.

8 Many scientists believe that these things and many others will one day be possible. But just because a thing is possible, is it *desirable*? Do you think that there should be strict laws about how far scientists can go with these sorts of experiments?

## Surrogate mothers

We are reading more and more in the press about couples who pay another woman to bear their child. This may happen because a woman is unable to bear children herself, or even when a couple are not prepared to disrupt their careers by going through pregnancy and birth.

The fertilised egg of a couple may be implanted into the womb of another woman who then bears the child and gives it to the 'biological' parents. In some cases, the surrogate donates her own egg. There is usually a written contract signed by the surrogate mother promising to hand over the child, usually in return for a considerable sum of money. Surrogate motherhood is becoming big business, and in America there are a number of agencies with women on their books who are prepared to offer their services to childless couples.

In English law a child born to a surrogate mother is regarded as illegitimate, and the surrogate mother is regarded as the natural mother.

---

### Something to discuss
What do you think about the following issues?

---

1 Many people disapprove of surrogate motherhood. They say that it makes children seem like goods to be bought in a shop. What is your opinion on this subject?

2 Are there any arguments in favour of the surrogate mother being allowed to keep the child if she has developed a strong attachment to it during pregnancy?

3 In 1985 the average 'price' for a baby was around £16000. This means that only the rich can afford to have a child by this means. If we accept surrogate motherhood, should it be a service supplied for all people, not just for the rich?

4 Why do you think that some people have such a desperate need for a child that they will go to any lengths to get one of their own?

5 Many people say that there is something seriously wrong with our values when we are at the same time aborting perfectly healthy babies who could be born and adopted, and also spending thousands of pounds on researching how to bring babies into the world who would otherwise not have been conceived. Give, with reasons, your opinion on this subject.

6 Some people are afraid that by experimenting in this way with human life we may disturb the balance of nature. In what ways might this balance be disturbed?

7 In a world where overpopulation is a growing problem, is it right that money from the health services should be spent on bringing more children into an already overcrowded world? Are there better uses for the money?

## The Warnock Report

Because so many people were concerned about the developments in research into fertility, the Government set up a committee to produce a report on the subject. There were sixteen people on the committee, representing doctors, scientists, lawyers and people of many religious persuasions. In June 1984 the report came up with these recommendations:

a) *Surrogate motherhood*
Fourteen members of the Committee were opposed to surrogate motherhood in principle, but everyone agreed that since the system does exist, it must be carefully watched. It was agreed that agencies making a profit out of 'baby sales' should be banned.

b) *'Test-tube babies'*
Hospitals carrying out this work are to be licensed and may be inspected at any time.

c) *AID*
All AID births should be registered. No man should father more than ten children. The identity of the donor is to be kept secret. AID children should be legitimate.

d) *Embryo research*
No embryo is to be allowed to develop 'in vitro' for more than fourteen days after fertilisation. All individual research on human embryos is to be licensed by a special committee.

## Transplants

A transplant takes place when a damaged organ, perhaps a heart or a kidney, is removed and replaced by one taken from another person. The 'spare part' may be taken from someone alive or dead. Kidneys are often taken from the living, because it is possible to live on one healthy kidney, but obviously things like hearts, livers, eyes and lungs have to be taken from the dead. The main *medical* problem is not that the actual operation is difficult but that the body is likely to reject 'foreign' tissue. People with transplanted organs have to be given large quantities of drugs to stop rejection, but even so most deaths after transplants are caused by rejection. The best results are obtained when the donor is a relative, or best of all, an identical twin.

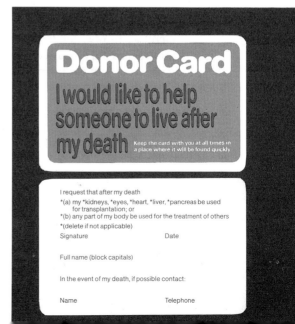

**Donor Card**
I would like to help someone to live after my death

Keep the card with you at all times in a place where it will be found quickly

I request that after my death
*(a) my *kidneys, *eyes, *heart, *liver, *pancreas be used
   for transplantation; or
*(b) any part of my body be used for the treatment of others
*(delete if not applicable)
Signature                    Date

Full name (block capitals)

In the event of my death, if possible contact:

Name                         Telephone

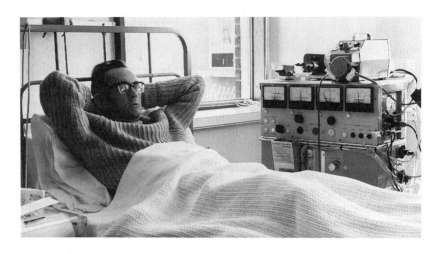

## Ethical problems

### Live donors

Some people say that it is not right to put at risk the life or health of one person in order to try to save the life of another. They also argue that the relatives of a patient needing a kidney transplant may be put under pressure to donate a kidney even if they do not really want to.

### Cadavers

A cadaver is the name given to a dead donor. The main ethical problem here is that organs have to be produced very quickly after death, and this raises the question, what is death? When does it occur? Also, it is argued, it is very upsetting for relatives who have just been informed of the death of a relative, to be asked almost immediately if organs may be used for transplants.

## What is death?

In the first part of this chapter we were asking 'when does life begin?' We now have to ask 'when does life end?'

### Brain death

A machine can now tell if all activity of the brain has stopped. Many doctors regard this as a sign of death, because all that remains is a body. No one will ever again find the 'person' that was once there.

### Clinical death

This is said to occur when the heart and lungs have ceased to work. The mechanics of the body have now ceased to function.

The matter is complicated by the use of machines. It has always been the case that a person who is 'clinically dead' can be revived – as in cases of drowning. If artificial respiration is given quickly enough, brain death can be avoided. But more confusingly, bodies can now be kept alive clinically for a long time after 'brain death' has occurred. The question is: *if a body is being kept alive by machines while the brain has ceased to function, is that person alive or dead? In fact, can they be considered a person at all?*

The reason why this question is connected with transplants is that some doctors prefer the bodies of donors to be kept artificially alive on machines up to the moment of transplant. But who is going to decide in this case whether a prospective donor is really dead? There is also the question of the doctor who desperately needs a new heart for a patient and who knows that a suitable donor has just been admitted on a respirator. Might he be tempted to diagnose death in the 'donor' where another doctor might not? It is very unlikely, but to guard against the possibility it has been decided that the doctor who declares the possible 'donor' dead must not be anyone to do with the transplant team. Also organs cannot be removed without the consent of relatives unless the donors have already signed documents saying that they wish their organs to be used.

---

**Something to discuss and write about**

1 What would be your feelings if you knew that after your death, parts of your body might be used to prolong the life of someone else, or improve the quality of their life?
2 Do you think that you would be prepared to give permission for the body of a relative to be used in this way?

---

*Who lives? ...*

One of the biggest problems about transplants is over who will be given one. There are far more people needing new kidneys for example than there are kidneys available for transplant, and the same applies to kidney machines which are also in short supply. Inevitably some people will go without – and sometimes this means that they will die. Yet again doctors have the unenviable task of deciding.

---

**Something to discuss and write about**

Transplants are very expensive. Some people say that the money spent on saving the lives of a few would be better spent on (for example) researching into the causes of heart disease or kidney failure, and so trying to prevent it. Do you agree with this point of view? Give reasons for your opinion.

---

*Money and medicine*

Saint Angela's hospital still has a sum of £20 000 which will be given for research to one of its big departments. Five of the hospital's leading doctors have been told to appear before the hospital's finance committee to put their case, and explain what they would do with the money if they were given it.

Divide into five groups. Each group is to take up the case of *one* of the following doctors, and one of the group should read the speech to the rest of the class. Then discuss to whom you would give the money if you were on the committee.

1 Dr Marsh is a specialist in infertility and wants money so that she can carry out research into human embryos which may help her understand why some men are infertile.

2 Dr Andrews wants the money to develop the work of his team who are doing further research into the effects of smoking on the internal organs.

3 Dr Wilson is a specialist in geriatric medicine. He wants the money to research into causes of senility in the elderly.

4 Dr Mohammed wants the money for his programme which investigates ways of preventing the rejection of transplanted organs.

5 Dr Isaacs wants the money to further her research into the causes and prevention of cot deaths.

---

### Something to discuss and write about

*Playing God . . .*

Another moral dilemma faces St Angela's. The hospital has just received another kidney dialysis machine. There are four patients in the hospital badly in need of dialysis. They are all equally sick, and each has an equally low chance of survival without dialysis. You are one of the team of four who decide which patient shall receive dialysis.

The patients are:

1 *Terry Bailey* Terry is 4 years old. He is the only child of Peter who is a chef, and Stacey who has a part-time cleaning job. Apart from the problem with his kidneys, Terry is physically quite strong.

2 *Dr Abdul Quaid* Doctor Quaid is researching the use of the sun's rays to produce power throughout the year at relatively low cost. Fellow scientists believe that he is near to success and that his work will lead to the development of a realistic alternative source of power to fossil-based fuels. This could be invaluable in many Third World countries as well as in the richer nations. Doctor Quaid is unmarried and his only relatives are his mother and sister who live in Pakistan.

3 *Jill Wheatley* Jill is the unemployed mother of four. When her kidney disease was diagnosed, her husband left her and the children. The children have now been taken into care, and Jill is in a poor state of health generally.

4 *Winston Weekes* Winston is a West Indian bus driver who came to Britain twenty years ago when he was 14. He is married with three children; is a leading member of his trade union and his local council. He is tipped to become Mayor next year.

Among the possible ways of deciding put forward by members of the team are these:

(a) that you 'draw lots' to decide.

(b) that since the decision will be unfair to three of the patients, no one shall have dialysis. Then at least all will receive equal treatment. Do you think these are valid ways of making the decision? What other ways might you use? State your final decision and the reasons for it.

# Euthanasia

Euthanasia literally means 'a good death'. It is a word used to describe a gentle and easy death and is applied to the killing of those who are incurably ill and in great pain and distress.

## *Voluntary euthanasia*

Voluntary euthanasia means bringing about death at the wish of the patient. It applies to people who would commit suicide if they could, but are unable to do so for physical reasons (e.g. they are paralysed). Under the present law, helping someone die, or killing them at their own request, is illegal, but a number of organisations are campaigning for this law to be changed. These organisations, such as EXIT and the Euthanasia Society, say that people should be allowed to decide when they die, and that people should be allowed to die a dignified death.

---

### *Something to discuss and write about*

You have just read about the opinion of pro-euthanasia groups. Here are some of the arguments put forward against voluntary euthanasia. What is your opinion?

---

1 *Religions arguments* The Bible says 'thou shalt not kill'. God should decide when life begins and when it ends. God works through people and he may have a purpose for the chronically sick, even though it may not be clear to us what this purpose is. Some people say that suffering is an important part of human experience. We must accept suffering with courage and try to learn from it, not try to run away from it.

2 *Moral arguments* Doctors are supposed to preserve life, not destroy it. (But Peter Singer writes: 'Once abortion is accepted, euthanasia lies around the next corner.')

3 *Humanitarian arguments* A person may say 'I want to die' in a moment of extreme agony, but not really mean it. Also, if euthanasia is made legal, many elderly people may be afraid to enter hospital. There is also the danger that elderly (and rich!) people who are chronically sick may be pressurised by relatives into asking for 'an easy way out'.

4 *Medical arguments* If we allow people to die when serious illness is diagnosed we will not have the chance to research into the illness and so prevent it happening later on. Also some very valuable work is being done in the area of terminal care (care for the dying). It is more worthwhile to develop this than to encourage premature death. Elizabeth Kubler Ross in her book *On Death and Dying* argues that given the right treatment and care, people can accept death and die without pain. Cecily Saunders writes, 'Euthanasia should be unnecessary and is an admission of defeat'.

*Non-voluntary euthanasia*

This term is applied when the person concerned is not capable of understanding the difference between life and death. It is usually applied to handicapped babies, but also to elderly and senile people.

Children with spina-bifida may suffer total or partial paralysis and mental handicap. Is such a life going to be so miserable that it would be kinder for doctors to let such children die rather than use surgery to keep them alive?

Downs Syndrome can be mild or serious. Is this child likely to cause so much distress to its parents or to other children in the family that it would be better if it were allowed to die? Does this child have a right to live, or should the parents who are responsible for its upbringing be the ones to decide its fate?

**Something to discuss and write about**
Do you think that physically and mentally handicapped children do have a chance of living a happy and fulfilled life? Is it really possible for anyone who is not handicapped to make this decision?

There are only too many occasions when as a result of road accidents people suffer terrible head injuries, as a result of which, large areas of the brain are destroyed and the person goes into a coma from which they are never likely to return. Such people can be 'kept alive' on respirators and intravenous feeding for months, even years.

At what point do you think that life-support machines should be turned off? Who should make the decision?

Anyone who has ever worked in a hospital, or has visited a ward with many elderly people in it, cannot have missed noticing the number of elderly patients who lie in bed, unable to feed themselves, clean themselves or communicate. They rely totally on nurses for their survival and comfort. No one knows why senility affects some elderly people and not others, but many people say that it is very degrading for the person involved, and that to die in such conditions is not a fitting end to a human life. It is argued that we keep humans alive under conditions in which we would put a much loved pet to sleep.

**Something to discuss and write about**
1 If euthanasia were made legal, doctors and relatives would often have to decide what was best for patients who were unable to speak for themselves. Without being in the patient's position, how well can they reach this decision?
2 When people lose any means of communication and seem to be totally unaware of their surroundings, how can we actually tell what is going on in their minds? How can we tell how happy or unhappy they are?
3 Once people are allowed to decide when others are to die, might there be dangers? Might euthanasia become a way of disposing of 'unwanted' people?

*A Christian attitude*
In 1965 the Church of England Board of Social Responsibility issued a report called *Decisions about Life and Death*. This report made the point that for Christians death is not a disaster, but a new beginning. Therefore attempts to preserve life at any cost were to be questioned. Patients whose days are numbered anyway should be allowed to die in peace, rather than spend their last weeks or months hooked to machinery or under the influence of powerful drugs.

## Christian hospices

As we have seen, people in favour of euthanasia argue that everyone should be allowed to die a 'dignified' death, rather than have to suffer months of physical and mental agony at the end. The hospice movement would actually agree with this ideal, although people who work in hospices do not regard euthanasia as the means of achieving this end.

Hospices are special hospitals which take care of the dying in their last few weeks of life. They take their name from the ancient hospices which were established in the Middle Ages to care for sick and dying pilgrims. Right from the start, hospices were concerned not only with the patient's physical wellbeing, but also with the state of mind, and one of the aims of the hospice is to help people to die at peace with themselves and with God.

Hospices try to put right some of the common criticisms of big general hospitals when it comes to caring for the dying. There is no feeling of failure for doctors, and no trying to avoid the questions and anxieties of the patients. In particular, whereas general hospital staff are told 'not to get involved' with the patients, involvement with the patient has become the hallmark of the hospice.

The aim of the hospice is to give the patient a 'good death'. The patients are seen as having a right to know about their condition, and because discussion with patients is such an important part of the work, all hospice workers, be they full-time or volunteer visitors, are properly trained in the care of the dying. The patient is helped to make his or her room as much like home as possible, and relatives are encouraged to visit and get involved with the work in hand until the very end. Most hospices have a Christian 'ethos' and many of the staff are likely to be Christians. One person always on call is the hospice chaplain. It is only natural that as they near the moment of death, people ask questions which they may have avoided for the rest of their lives: 'What has been the purpose of my life?' 'What is going to happen to me?' 'Why is this happening to me?' A chaplain will not know all the answers but will be able to help the person talk through their own solutions.

Hospices place a heavy emphasis on pain relief. We all know that when we are in severe pain we are not ourselves, and we are certainly not at peace with ourselves or our surroundings. Hospices use narcotics to stop pain arising. Used often but in small quantities they enable the patient to stay alert. The patient may become addicted to the drug, but in the last few weeks of life that hardly matters.

Few people who have come into contact with a hospice have failed to be impressed by their atmosphere and philosophy. Such contacts have often given people new insights into life and human existence. Elizabeth Kubler Ross, one of Britain's most experienced hospice doctors, writes:

To be a therapist to a dying patient makes us aware of the uniqueness of each individual in the vast sea of humanity. . . . Few of us live beyond our three score years and ten, and yet in that brief time most of us create and live a happy biography and weave ourselves into the fabric of human history.

(*On Death and Dying*, Tavistock Press, 1977)

You can find a list of British hospices, many of which will arrange for visitors to speak at your school, or will send you pamphlets for project work, in the back of *The Hospice Alternative* by Margaret Manning (Condor, 1984).

# 6 Settling arguments

He was always picking fights with the other children, and because he was a big boy, he often hurt them quite badly. Once when I saw him fighting in the playground I took him inside, and after leaving him to cool off for a bit, I asked him if he was sorry. He said that he was sorry, but after we'd chatted for a bit, it became clear that his regrets were not that he hurt people, but that I'd stopped the fight before he'd had a chance to win it and show the others what a 'big man' he was.    (A primary school teacher)

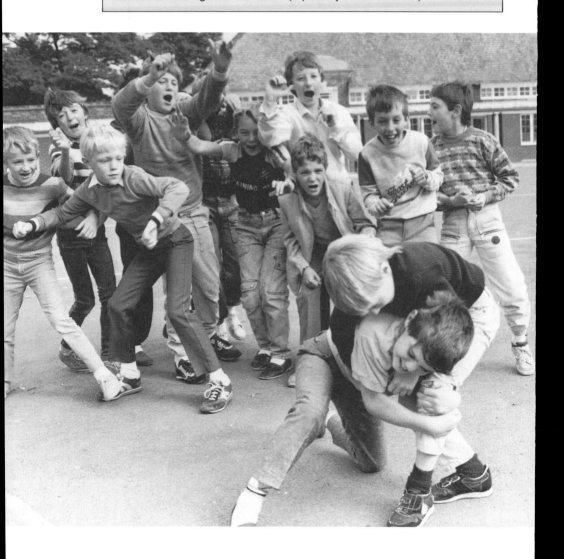

**Something to discuss and write about**

1 Do you think that human beings have a basic instinct to fight? If so, is this instinct the same in boys and in girls?

2 If we do have an instinct to fight, should we try to suppress it?

3 Do you think that children and /or adults admire those who are physically 'tough'? If so, why?

4 Can you think of a situation where:
   (a)  You have used physical violence or wanted to use it?
   (b)  Someone has used physical violence against you?

Discuss any incidents which members of the class remember. Did the use of violence solve the problem in any of these cases?

Discuss ways in which these situations could have been solved without the use of violence.

### The use of violence

There are many situations where human beings use physical force against each other. Here are seven typical situations where violence might be used. In each case try to think of a specific example to illustrate the point. The first one has been done for you.

Violence is often used . . .

1 by individuals to further their own ends, e.g. a thief may attack the owner of a shop before robbing it.

2 by an individual in self-defence.

3 by an individual in the defence of others.

4 by a group to achieve their own ends.

5 by a group in self-defence.

6 by a group in defence of others.

7 by a whole nation when they give authority to their leaders to:
   (a)  use torture, capital punishment, or corporal punishment.
   (b)  seek to expand their territories.
   (c)  protect their interests abroad.
   (d)  defend themselves against an aggressor.
   (e) go to the aid of an ally who is being invaded.

Violence begins with the individual, and it is with the individual that any moves towards peace can begin. This is why many people believe that peace studies should be taught in school so that the adults of tomorrow can be taught the consequences of violence and possible ways in which ordinary people can help to create peace in our time.

*Teach your children to forgive; make your homes places of love and reconciliation. It would be a crime against youth and their future to let any child grow up with nothing but the experience of violence and hate*

(Pope John Paul II)

> **Something to discuss and write about**
> 1 Do you think that parents should teach their children to 'stick up for themselves'? If so, can children be taught to do this without the use of physical force?
> 2 Some people think that there should be a ban on the manufacture of war games and videos, toy soldiers and guns, etc. Do you think that such toys and games encourage children to be violent?
> 3 Do you think that peace studies should be taught in school?

## *Emotional violence*

It is not only by the use of physical force that we hurt each other. 'Emotional cruelty' has in the past been grounds for divorce, and many teachers and social workers could tell stories of children who are emotionally battered. What sort of things do you believe come under the heading of 'emotional cruelty'?

For example, do you agree that 'Sticks and stones may hurt my bones, but names will never hurt me'?

## The teaching of religions about violence

It is certainly not true to say that only religious people are opposed to the use of violence, but it is true that most religions of the world do preach non-violence, even if this teaching is not always observed by the followers of those religions.

## *Buddhism on violence*

Buddhism teaches the eight noble truths which are seen as a guide to life. The third of these, concerning 'right speech', says that speech should be kindly and reconciling, that people should not gossip or backbite. The fourth noble truth teaches about 'right action' and puts forward the principle of *ahimsa* (non-violent action) also found in other Eastern religions. There are particularly strict rules for Buddhist

monks who are told that 'anger must be overcome by the absence of anger; evil must be overcome by good'. Monks are not allowed to kill animals for meat. On the subject of using violence against other people, monks are told to reflect that should someone attack them, the attacker harms his own inner being by his action, and that if you bear a grudge against an attacker or fight against him in return, your own inner peace will be destroyed.

> Look at the person who takes up a stick. By this action he creates fear in himself. . . . Hatred is not conquered by hatred; hatred is conquered by love.                                                                    (Shakyamuni Buddha)

## Christianity on violence

There can be no doubt that Jesus himself did not use violence, nor would he let others use violence in his defence. When he was in the Garden of Gethsemane, and one of his disciples attacked a guard, Jesus stopped him saying, 'Those who live by the sword, die by the sword.' There was every reason why Jesus should not use violence in self-defence, since he regarded it as part of his mission that he should 'die for the people'. Some Christians say that his followers today should bear this fact in mind when considering how far they should go in applying Jesus' principles to their own lives. Not everyone has to die for the salvation of mankind: so perhaps Christians do not have to follow Jesus' example in this matter?

However, Jesus did set out a very positive example for non-violent living. Look up the following passages and answer these questions.

1 Matthew 5:21–6. Why do you think that Jesus said that hating people was as bad as killing them?
2 Matthew 5:38–42. Is this advice always practical? Think of situations in which following this advice would, and would not, be the right thing to do.
3 Matthew 5:43–8. What do you think 'love' means in this context?
4 Romans 12:27–31. What do you think Paul means here when he says, 'by doing so you will heap live coals on his head'?

## Civil protest and revolution

Much of the violence in the world today is not caused by countries fighting each other, but by groups within a country opposing their governments. The governments dislike the activity of these groups and call them 'guerillas', 'rebels' or 'extremists'. However, most groups of this kind regard their cause as just. Christians are as likely to be involved in opposition to the state as anyone else – as, for example, those who oppose many of the regimes in South America, those who oppose the South African government, and those fighting on both sides in Northern Ireland. Many people say that Christians should not oppose the state, and that Christianity should 'keep out of politics' in general.

*Christians and the powers-that-be*

The Bible holds very mixed views about obedience to the state.

Old Testament writers do not always show much respect for their kings and political leaders. They did, however, respect the prophets, who were seen as God's spokesmen. It is not uncommon to find in the Old Testament, stories about prophets who plot to remove kings who are seen as disobedient to God's will. Two prophets in particular are said to have played an important part in the replacement of an 'unsuitable' king by one who was more suitable. See 1 Samuel 15:26–8; and 1 Kings 21:20–26.

In the New Testament there is no evidence that Jesus plotted to remove either Herod Antipas the king, or the Roman governor, even though he probably had little time for Antipas who showed no respect for the law or for human life. Yet Jesus lived in violent times, and it is possible that some of his followers hoped that he would become a rebel leader against the occupying Roman forces. If so, they were disappointed, because Jesus, like the Pharisees of his day, taught his hearers to find personal fulfilment in the development of their personal and spiritual lives, not in political action. Jesus is not on record as having said anything about war or revolution, although some people think that the parable of the wicked tenants (Matt. 21:33–46) was meant to teach that rebellion against Rome would result in the removal of the Jewish government and its replacement by complete Roman rule.

Read the following passages. What do they tell us about Jesus' attitude towards the use of force, and his attitude towards the state?

Matt. 4:1–11; Matt. 19:1–11 (cf. Zechariah 9:9); Matt. 19:12–13; Matt. 12:17ff

The Christian communities which sprang up after Jesus' death lived in an equally dangerous world. At first the Palestinian Church faced opposition from the Jewish leaders, but as the Church spread, it came up against a far more formidable enemy – the Roman Empire. The Romans were tolerant of any group who would worship the gods of Rome as well as their own. (The Jews were especially privileged not to have to worship the Roman gods.) But by the second century most Christians were no longer Jewish, but were ordinary Romans, and as such were expected to toe the party line. Whenever the Empire was threatened by plague, invasion, flood or drought, or any calamity, everyone was expected to offer sacrifices to the gods as a sign of loyalty to the state. When large numbers of Christians refused to do this, they were killed. In vain did Christian writers like Justin and Tertullian write to the emperors trying to persuade them that Christians were loyal. Even as early as New Testament times Christians had been trying to convince the authorities that they were not traitors – they just refused to worship any other god but their own.

**Passages for discussion**

1 1 Tim. 2:1–2.
   (a) Name two religions in Britain which say prayers for the government and the royal family in their public worship?
   (b) Why do you think that many religious services contain prayers for the state?
2 Romans 13:1–7.
   (a) What sort of duty to the government do you think Paul had in mind here?
   (b) In what situations, if any, might it be difficult to apply this attitude?

## Is it ever right to oppose the state?

Some people say that all authority comes from God, and that Christians should never oppose those who have been placed in positions of authority. Others, however, say that men and women are put in power by people, and that if they act unjustly, Christians – like anyone else – have a duty to protest, although not necessarily with violence. To do nothing when you see people being treated unjustly is like agreeing with the policy of the oppressor, it is argued. A German writer put it like this:

> First they came for the Jews, and I did not speak out because I wasn't a Jew.
> Then they came for the Communists and I didn't speak out because I wasn't a Communist.
> Then they came for the trade unionists, but I didn't speak out because I wasn't a trade unionist.
> Then they came for me; and there was no one left to speak out for me.
>
> (Pastor Niemoller)

## Protest

All over the world people want to live in peace. But because many of them live in countries which deny them human rights, many people feel that they must protest against injustice. Even in democratic countries, minority groups are sometimes not adequately represented at government level. Some people would agree that this is the case in Britain with, for example, the black community, the poor and the unemployed. But in Britain at least there are legal means of expressing discontent – through demonstrations, writing to the press, voting and so on. But still many people feel that this does not achieve very much for those who suffer injustice, and sometimes they resort to violence out of sheer frustration with their situation, as happened in Toxteth and Brixton.

## Violent protest

After years of suffering under *apartheid*, some of the black population of South Africa turned to violence. The World Council of Churches was criticised for sending money which was used to support this cause.

*An IRA bomb kills three people and injures many others in this attempt to wipe out the entire British cabinet in 1984.*

When Hitler came to power in Germany, he decided on the 'final solution' to the Jewish presence in Germany. He also introduced euthanasia programmes for the disabled and mentally ill. Many people, some of them Christians, defied the government and helped Jewish families to escape. One of Hitler's opponents was Dietrich Bonhoeffer, a Lutheran Minister, who was one of a number of Christians involved in plots to assassinate Hitler.

### Something to discuss and write about

1 What evidence is there that the use of violence in these cases has drawn people's attention to the causes being represented?

2 Do you think that the use of violence has brought success or popularity for any of these causes?

3 Do you feel any sympathy towards any of these people for their opposition to the state? Do you feel that any of them were right to use violence? Give reasons for your answer.

4 The press tend to report acts of violence. Why do you think they do this? Might press coverage create more publicity for their cause?

Some Christians believe that there can be no peace without justice, and that if we want peace, we must work to remove the causes of violence. Some believe with Bonhoeffer that there are times when the use of violence can be justified.

*Christian Peace Conference*
The Christian Peace Conference of 1966 declared that Christians might participate in violent revolution if:
1 Violence has already been used by the oppressor.
2 All legal means of opposition have been tried without success.
3 The results of revolution would be less harmful to human life than are the present policies of the oppressor.
    Do you agree with these reasons?

## Non-violent protest
As a rule violence makes the headlines, but non-violence often does not. (Why do you think this is?) This may lead some people to believe that the only way of protesting is by using violence. However, all over the world there are people who are busy working out peaceful ways of settling arguments, believing that only in this way will the world ever find peace.

---

**Research**

Find out about the non-violent protest of:
Mahatma Gandhi; Martin Luther King Jr; Leo Tolstoy; George Fox;
Danielo Dolci; Helder Camara.

---

*Working for peace*
Many people have been inspired by the work of Martin Luther King and Gandhi to persevere in non-violent protest. For example, when in 1970 plans were made to extend an army camp over an area of France where the 'peasant' farmers of Larzac grazed their sheep, a peaceful protest began which was to last for several years. The farmers were supported by a number of priests and laity of the Catholic Church.
    The protest began with prayers and fasting. People from all over France came to join in. In 1972 two demonstrations made the headlines: the first when 103 tractors were driven to Rodez, and the second, when the citizens of Paris woke up one morning to the sight of sheep with 'Save the Larzac' printed on their fleeces, grazing under the Eiffel Tower! In 1973, 26 farmers drove their tractors to Paris, gaining tremendous support as they travelled.
    Back in the Larzac in 1974, wheat was grown for Upper Volta which was suffering a famine at the time. This was to make the point that military expansion was on this occasion at the cost of feeding the hungry. Then in 1975 a Peace Study centre was set up in the area which went on to gain international acclaim.

The climax to the campaign came in 1981 when the farmers wrote to all the candidates in the forthcoming general election, asking them about their policy on Larzac. Francois Mitterand said that he would cancel the plans for the new military base altogether, and less than a month after his victory he carried out this promise.

Larzac became known all over the world as a symbol of peaceful protest, and there is hope that other people who feel that they are fighting for a just cause can learn from the patience of the French farmers.

Roger Rawlinson writes:

> They started off with the idea of simply defending their land . . . but soon realised that their problem was not unique. They discovered that many people throughout the world were, in many cases, suffering from worse injustices than they were through the abuse of governmental power and increasing militarization. They learned how effective nonviolent action can be in obtaining more control over their lives and ended up as participants in a growing movement for justice and peace.
>
> (*Larzac: A Victory for Non-violence*)

## Corrymeela

Corrymeela is a small settlement near Ballycastle in County Antrim, in Northern Ireland. In 1965 it was purchased by a small group of people who wanted to establish a community of Christians from all denominations, Catholic and Protestant alike. Later they also bought a house – now Corrymeela House – in Belfast.

Members of the community are of all ages, from all backgrounds, and belong to all branches of the Church in Ireland. The aims of the community are to teach people to live in peace and to establish a just community in Northern Ireland. The community members feel that they have all been called to be 'instruments of God's peace'.

The aims of the community are:
– to bring Catholics and Protestants together
– to care for those who suffer violence
– to break down the barriers of mistrust and fear
– to increase understanding and tolerance
– to work for justice in society
– to lay the foundations of peace.

Activities centre on Corrymeela itself, the house in Belfast and the homes of community members. The centre acts as a place where individuals and groups can go to get away from the tensions and violence of city life, meet others of different beliefs, discuss, work and play with them in an atmosphere of peace. There are youth camps, work camps, courses on social responsibility and holidays for those in need. Over 6000 young people take part in these activities every year, and these are the people on whom the future of Northern Ireland depends. The hope is that in an atmosphere of peace and under-standing, individuals will lose their prejudices and learn to build relationships with those whom they have traditionally regarded as the enemy. They can then take home with them all the lessons they have learnt, and hopefully influence their communities towards establishing peace.

## The Corrymeela Link

Corrymeela has fired the imagination of people living outside Ireland, and they have formed an organisation known as the Corrymeela Link which has its headquarters in Reading. Corrymeela is not seen as having all the answers to the problems which cause violence, but many people feel that peace will only spread throughout the world as a result of the efforts of ordinary men and women who are tired of waiting for governments to solve their problems. Most of its supporters believe that we cannot be *told* to love our enemies. We must *experience* coming to terms with the 'enemy' by living and working with them. If some individuals can do this, they can go home and teach their families and friends that it is possible. A lot of people see the methods used at Corrymeela as a possible solution to other violent situations in the world. Not surprisingly, Corrymeela investigates the causes of violence, realising that violence and tension can only be remedied when the causes have been removed. Racism, unemployment and the arms trade are all seen as primary causes of dissatisfaction and violence.

## Neve Shalom

Neve Shalom is a settlement not unlike Corrymeela, but for very different people. Neve Shalom was set up in Israel by Father Bruno Husar in 1978 as a cooperative village where Jews, Christians and Muslims can show the world that it is possible for them to live in peace.

Neve Shalom means 'Oasis of Peace', and the community was set up with the idea that families could hold their own religion while respecting that of others. As at Corrymeela, the emphasis is very much on youth, and in 1979, a peace school was set up. The activities of the school include work camps, seminars and summer schools for equal numbers of Jews and Arabs. Those who go there tend to be not very orthodox, and there is as much if not more interest now in bringing together Jews and Arabs as political groups rather than Jews and Muslims as religious groups.

Languages and customs often prove to be barriers between people of different races, so people who go to Neve Shalom learn each others' languages, eat each others' food, and observe each others' customs. As with Corrymeela there are constant visits from people outside Israel who want to learn the ways of peace. Much of the money which supports Neve Shalom comes from Europe and America.

Although the people at Neve Shalom come from backgrounds very different from those at Corrymeela, politically the situation in Northern Ireland is not so very different from that in Israel. In both cases a dominant governing group is seen to have oppressed the other, and this has led to intense hatred in both cases. Neither at Corrymeela nor at Neve Shalom is there any illusion that peace can come purely from good will. Peace can only come if people feel that they are treated with equal justice.

---

**Something to discuss and write about**

1 Corrymeela and Neve Shalom concentrate on teaching non-violence to the young. Why do you think this is?
2 Can you think of any other conflict situations which might be helped by the sort of approach taken at Corrymeela and Neve Shalom?
3 Do you think that ordinary people have a better chance than do politicians of achieving peace in places like Northern Ireland? If so, why should this be?
4 What sort of people might not like Corrymeela-type projects?

---

## War and peace

Most people condemn those who use violence – unless they are wearing a uniform. It is generally accepted that when there is a war, members of the armed forces may kill. Even in peacetime, some people are 'licensed to kill', for some policemen and secret servicemen carry guns, and use them.

### Pacifism

There are some people who refuse to use violence under any circumstances. They are called pacifists. Most people become aware of pacifists during wartime; indeed, some people may not become aware that they are themselves pacifists until their call-up papers arrive. During wartime, pacifists have been subjected to ridicule, have been regarded as traitors or cowards, and imprisoned as conscientious objectors.

*Types of pacifism*
Not all pacifists have the same reasons for their beliefs. These are some of them.

1 Pacifism of principle:
Pacifists of this type say that 'on principle' the only way to secure peace is to refuse ever to use violence. They might argue that once you make one exception to this rule, you open the floodgates and many other exceptions will be found. Christian pacifists of principle follow the example of Jesus and the Christian martyrs, saying that non-violence leads ultimately to victory.

2 Pragmatic pacifism:
Pragmatic pacifists say that they reached the conclusion that pacifism is the most moral course purely on rational grounds, i.e. they worked it out through rational argument. They argue that the results of the use of violence are so severe that using violence cannot be in anyone's interest.

3 Selective objection:

There are probably more pacifists in this category than in any other. Selective objectors do not refuse to use violence under *all* circumstances, but only under *some*. For example, many Americans refused to fight in the Vietnam war because they said that it was not a just war. There are many people who would refuse to fight in a war in which nuclear weapons might be used, on the same grounds.

> ### Something to discuss and write about
> See what you think about the following.

*Arguments in favour of pacifism*

Here are some of the common arguments used by pacifists to support their case. Do you agree with these arguments? How would you argue against them?

1 'Violence leads to violence.' When violence is used, those who are attacked are often frightened into using violence themselves.
2 Jesus said, 'Blessed are the peacemakers', 'Thou shalt not kill' and 'Do not repay evil for evil'. Some Christian pacifists say that no one who claims to be a Christian can be anything *but* pacifist.
3 Other Christians claim that pacifism is a vocation for some, but that not all Christians should be expected to be pacifists.
4 Many people argue for pacifism on economic grounds. Over £100 000 000 000 million a year is spent on weapons of war – money which could be spent improving the quality of life for millions of people.
5 In the end, history has shown that it is the men and women of peace who are remembered and admired for their work; people like Gandhi, Luther King and Mother Teresa.

*Arguments against pacifism*

Do you agree with these arguments? How would you argue against them?

1 Most Christians are not pacifists. Some of them argue that although Jesus himself did not use violence, he never said anything about fighting wars. Using violence as an individual may be wrong, but fighting in a war is not necessarily so. Also, Jesus had to die for the salvation of the world. This does not apply to the rest of us.
2 Jesus talked of the Kingdom of God in terms of peace and love. But until the Kingdom is established we have to live in *this* world. It may be the case that people do not start fights in God's kingdom, but they do in our world. What all pacifists must ask themselves is this: 'If I see a man aiming a machine gun at a playground full of children, and I am able to overcome him by using force, will I do it?'
3 Jesus taught us to love our neighbour. Is it 'loving' to see an

individual or group being attacked by an aggressor and do nothing about it?

4 When your country is at war, thousands of people are dying to secure your freedom and way of life. Is it not selfish and irresponsible to let them do this for you, when you yourself are safely at home?

---

**Summary questions**

1 If Britain were to go to war, would you be prepared to fight?
2 If you accept that war is justified, should women fight as well as men?
3 Ministers of religion are exempt from military action. Should this exemption be extended to all religious people?

---

*Pacifism and the Quakers*

There is one particular Christian group which includes pacifism as one of its basic beliefs. This is the Society of Friends, or the Quakers as they are better known.

The Quaker peace testimony was presented to Charles II in 1660:

> We utterly deny all outward wars and strife, and fighting with outward weapons, for any end, or under any pretence whatsoever; this is our testimony to the whole world. The Spirit of Christ by which we are guided is not changeable, so as once to command us to a thing as evil, and again to move unto it; and we certainly know and testify to the world, that the Spirit of Christ, which leads us into all truth, will never move us to fight a war against any man with outward weapons, neither for the kingdom of Christ, nor for the kingdoms of the world.

More recently, they have said:

> Our renunciation of violence requires a positive effort to encourage and promote non-violent opposition to oppression, which is the only real and lasting means of true liberation. . . . Positive and effective non-violence is the alternative we offer to warfare . . . what price are we prepared to pay for peace?

> (*A Quaker Peace Testimony for Today*, 1978)

## War in religious traditions

*Hinduism and war*

The doctrine of *ahimsa* is common to Hindus, Buddhists and Jains. Ahimsa means 'non-harmfulness' and 'non-violence'. Some Hindus live by this principle, some do not.

The most famous exponent of the doctrine of Ahimsa was Gandhi who said that violence was the law of wild animals. But humans have a spirit which should call them to a higher way. According to Gandhi, refusing to use violence is not to submit to suppression and tyranny.

Rather, it is a demonstration of strength and power by someone who is prepared to suffer for what is right.

### Buddhism and war

According to the five precepts for monks and lay people, Buddhists are not supposed to take life. But in modern times this teaching has been modified. In Vietnam, Buddhist monks tried to oppose the war by non-violent means, and a number of them burnt themselves alive in protest against the war. But in other parts of the East, Buddhists have been known to fight for certain causes.

### Judaism and war

Parts of the Tenach encourage the use of violence, and a number of early narratives tell of how God 'commanded' the Israelites to destroy their enemies. In the centuries after the tribes occupied Palestine, there grew up the tradition of 'Holy War' when the Israelites believed that God was fighting at their head, enthroned on the Ark of the Covenant. Yet there are also stories in the Tenach which encourage love for the enemy, and a desire for wars to cease. In the later books there is stress on trusting in God rather than in weapons of war (Isaiah 30:15–16; Psalm 33:16), and in the books of Isaiah and Micah we find one of the most beautiful descriptions of peace for all time.

It is from Judaism that the world has gained the word *shalom*, meaning peace, and later Jewish tradition as expressed in the Talmud, makes peace a central goal in life. The Jews have endured centuries of persecution, and today Jewish attitudes towards violence vary from the militant Zionists who believe in fighting for the state of Israel, to those who believe that 'reward is in proportion to one's sufferings' and accept suffering as a vocation and testimony to their faith.

### Christianity and war

Until the fourth century AD the majority of Christians did not fight in the army or take public office. But as Christianity became the official religion of the Roman Empire, and virtually everyone was Christian, at least in name, it became accepted that only the clergy were exempt from military service. Indeed religion and patriotism went hand in hand; a tradition which has persisted in Britain to this day.

Do you know where these excerpts come from?

Wider still and wider, shall thy bounds be set;
God who made thee mighty, make thee mightier yet.

O Lord our God arise,
Scatter his enemies
And make them fall
Confound their politics
Frustrate their knavish tricks ...

*Islam and war*
The word 'Islam' comes from an Arabic root 'silm' which means peace, purity, obedience or submission. Muslims believe that peace will come to the world when all people submit to God and his will.

We saw when we were considering the place of women in religious communities that Western people often form their impressions of Islam from reports in the press and on television of dramatic but isolated events in the Muslim world. So we hear and read about groups of 'Muslim fundamentalists' or 'Islamic terrorists' committing acts of violence against their enemies. We are also beginning to hear that such groups think of themselves as engaging in 'Holy War'. However, the activities of these groups are no more representative of the beliefs of Islam as a whole than are the activities of the IRA representative of Christian attitudes. The idea of peace is central to Islam, just as it is to the majority of people of other faiths.

There are frequent misunderstandings of the concept of 'Jihad', which is often translated as 'Holy War' but which means 'striving in God's path'. The idea behind Jihad is that the Muslim community should strive against outward and inner evil and corruption. The majority of Muslims regard Jihad as 'inner striving'. This means that the main purpose of Jihad is to 'fight' against the dangers which might make their society break away from the principles taught by Islam.

The use of violence remains an issue over which people of all religious persuasions, and none, find it very difficult to relate their ideals to what is practical. The usual argument has been, 'I don't want to fight, but if the other side starts it, what am I to do?'

## The just war
The idea of the just war developed within the Christian tradition and has affected the thinking of Europe, at least, for hundreds of years. Some people, as we have seen, do not believe that there can be such a thing as a just war, but others, probably the majority of people who think about it, judge the morality of each war by the following rules, which have become known as the rules for fighting a just war.

1 The war must be declared on the authority of the rightful rulers of the country.
2 The cause must be just.
3 Those who fight must do so with the right intention, which is to bring about good and destroy evil.
4 War must have been the last resort. All methods of peaceful settlement through diplomacy and other means must have been tried first.
5 The good achieved as the result of war must outweigh the evil which led to the war.

6 War may be fought only if there is a reasonable chance of success.
7 War must be fought by proper means. This means adopting the
following two principles:
  (a) 'Proportionality'. The amount of force used must not be out of
      proportion to the needs of the situation, i.e. to use only as
      much force as you need, and no more.
  (b) 'The principle of double effect'. This refers to the side-effects of
      war. The principle states that it is permissible to cause side-
      effects to war if the cause is strong enough. For example, if in
      order to wipe out an enemy base of vital strategic importance
      you have to kill some civilians as well, then you may do it. The
      'Dambuster' bombings of the Second World War might be
      given as a good example of this principle. In order to cripple
      German military industry, major dams in Holland were des-
      troyed, inevitably causing loss of life to civilian allies.

---

**Something to discuss and write about**

1 Look at the criteria for a just war. Do you agree that a war fought on
these principles could be just? Give reasons for your answer.
2 What do you consider to be a just cause for war?
3 Ask members of your class who study history to give an account of any
wars they have been studying. Discuss the causes of these wars, and
see if you can think of any ways in which the disputes could have been
solved without the use of violence.

---

### For Queen and country

There is nothing like a war to make even a nominally Christian
country like Britain forget the commandment, 'But I say to you, love
your enemies and pray for those who persecute you.' However much
we may pride ourselves on our right of free speech and freedom of
opinion, when a war breaks out there is a general understanding that
we toe the party line, support the war effort and stand firmly behind
our government and our fighting troops. In times of war pacifists may
be regarded as traitors, as may those who question the justice of the
cause. We have seen how in the Second World War people like
Bonhoeffer conspired with the enemy (Britain) and even plotted to
kill their head of state and bring about a quick agreement with the
Allies. Bonhoeffer has been remembered as a martyr and a man of
principle. But how would we feel if a British person acted in the same
way?

It is very difficult to follow your conscience in time of war. There
are tremendous pressures on all of us to adopt the attitude of the
majority, and for anyone who doubts whether the cause is just there
must always be the nagging question, 'Everyone else seems to think
the cause is just. What makes me so sure that I'm right?'

A good example of the sort of argument that goes on in time of war can be seen from the Falklands war. On Friday, 22 April 1982 Argentine troops invaded the Falkland Islands, forcing the British military garrison there to surrender. Over the following days there were heated arguments in and out of Parliament as to how Britain should respond to this invasion of what we regarded as our territory. A task force was sent to the South Atlantic which eventually recaptured the islands.

To many of us, the fact that we were at war seemed unbelievable. There were no bombs dropped over London, no food rationing, no blackouts, and apart from those families who had relatives in the task force, life went on much as usual. Many people in Britain did not know where the Falkland Islands were. As for Argentina, it was a country we played in the World Cup, although many people were aware that it was run by a military junta with a very bad record on human rights.

Some people thought that whatever were the rights and wrongs of engaging in war with Argentina, now that we were committed to war, we should put our personal doubts behind us and support the war effort. After all, what could be more discouraging to 'our boys' than to read in the papers that there were people in Britain who did not agree with the cause for which they were risking, and in some cases giving, their lives?

Nevertheless there were people in Britain who did question the justice of the war. Some believed that the islands should not have been captured by Argentina so easily, and that now the lives of British servicemen were being risked over a matter of pride – to teach Argentina that Britain could not be pushed around. From the very beginning, the war in the South Atlantic was matched by the war at home. This 'war of words' was waged particularly between two of Britain's most popular newspapers, the *Mirror* and the *Sun*.

Look at the following excerpts and discuss:

(a) the views being expressed
(b) The effect that such arguments might have on the minds and emotions of readers.

MIGHT ISN'T RIGHT
The main purpose of British policy should now be to get the best possible settlement for the Islanders. We could probably throw the Argentines out of the Falklands but for how long?

. . . The islands don't matter. The people do. We should offer each of them the chance to settle here or anywhere they choose, and we should pay for it . . . the Argentine invasion has humiliated the government. But military revenge is not the way to wipe it out . . .

Calculating and miscalculating politicians started this conflict. Now it is time to end it. Now is the time for politicians to risk their reputation and find peace. Their biographies should not be written in the blood of others. . . . Peace through diplomacy is the only policy that pays.

(*Mirror*, 5 May 1982)

In response to the scathing attack by the *Sun* claiming that the *Mirror* was unpatriotic, the *Mirror* replied that patriotism does not have to be proved in blood, 'especially someone else's blood'. The following extract is from the *Sun*, and concerns discussions about sending the task force to the South Atlantic:

> For ourselves we do not care where it (the Foreign Office) finds its recruits ... provided they have fire in their bellies and a determination in their heart that no one is going to push Britain around.... NOTHING comes ahead of the people of Britain, their lives, their prosperity, their future.

On the idea of a negotiated settlement, the *Sun* said:

STICK IT UP YOUR JUNTA:

To promote national participation in the war effort it offered:

> £5 for every Argie Bargie joke
> Are you feeling shirty with the enemy? Want to give those dam Argies a whole lot of bargie?
> Course you do! Well – here's your chance to put your feelings up front.
> Our 'STICK IT UP YOUR JUNTA' T shirt is a sensational reminder of the most popular headline to come out of the Falklands fight.

After a British submarine torpedoed the Argentine cruiser *General Belgrano* with the loss of many Argentine lives, a headline in the *Sun* said:

GOTCHA!

The battle of words was not confined to the newspapers. The BBC was also involved. During the war the BBC used sources of information from Argentina and the USA in presenting its bulletins. In an attempt to present facts objectively it used the terms 'the Argentines' and 'the British' rather than 'the enemy' and 'our forces'. Some people complained that the BBC was presenting the war as being fought between two equal forces and behaving like a neutral onlooker. Some people were also angry at the sympathy shown on *Panorama* for Argentine casualties.

## The nuclear debate

Attitudes towards war have changed considerably since the Second World War, as a result of the introduction of nuclear weapons. At the end of the last war, the USA dropped atomic bombs on Hiroshima and Nagasaki to bring about a quick surrender from Japan. This device was only successful because Japan did not possess nuclear weapons with which to retaliate. It is very unlikely that such a situation could occur again, for any country which now has nuclear weapons is a likely target for other countries with similar weapons.

Once the effect of nuclear weapons had been seen at Hiroshima and Nagasaki, other countries wanted them. No country wanted ever to find itself without nuclear weapons and under attack from a

country which did have them. Thus began the nuclear 'arms race'. Many countries, including Britain, are constantly trying to keep up with, and if possible overtake, their 'enemies' in the power, range and accuracy of their nuclear weapons. We now possess between us enough of these weapons to destroy the planet several times over, and many people, especially the young, feel anger and frustration at a situation which they did not create, do not want, and yet seem powerless to change.

*Aspiring sincerely to an international peace based on justice and order, the Japanese people forever renounce war as a sovereign right of the nation and the threat or use of force as a means of settling international disputes.* (Article 9 of Japan's post-war constitution)

*What are nuclear weapons?*

Everything·in life is made up of atoms which consist of protons and neutrons. A nuclear weapon explodes as a result of either *fission* or *fusion*, or both. Nuclear fission is the splitting of an atom of uranium or plutonium. When this happens, a chain reaction is set up, and atoms go on splitting, resulting in a huge release of energy. Nuclear fusion happens when, as a result of intense heat (commonly caused by nuclear fission), two light nuclei of deuterium or tritium (forms of hydrogen) join together. *Thermonuclear bombs* (hydrogen bombs) are some of the most powerful, since they produce fission and fusion. *Neutron bombs* have a high level of radiation but give off little blast and fall out. This means that they kill life forms but do less harm to buildings.

Today there is a vast range of nuclear weapons. Britain as a member of NATO has a number of US air and nuclear submarine bases. Britain also has an *independent deterrent* which in 1985 consisted of four Polaris submarines in Scotland. But there are plans to replace Polaris with Trident at the cost $10 000 million. There are also plans for Britain to take delivery of more US cruise missiles which are small unmanned aircraft carrying nuclear warheads. They are very mobile and can even be launched from the backs of lorries.

*Disarmament*

All over the world people are working for peace – between individuals, between groups, between nations. Some organisations such as CND (Campaign for Nuclear Disarmament) concentrate on plans for disarmament. Some people want nuclear disarmament, others want disarmament of conventional weapons as well.

Two terms are commonly used in connection with disarmament:

*Multilateral disarmament* means that all nations should work to reduce arms together. People who favour multilateral disarmament say that it is only reasonable to get rid of our nuclear weapons if the Russians and other potential enemies do as well.

*Unilateral disarmament* Supporters of unilateral disarmament say that since the nuclear powers have proved themselves unable to reduce their weaponry working together, someone must take the lead and go it alone to show that they are genuine in their desire for peace. Most CND members support unilateral disarmament. They want Britain to be like Norway and Denmark who refuse to have nuclear weapons on their soil in peacetime.

One form of unilateralism, known as staged unilateralism, was proposed by an American, Charles Osgood, in his book *An Alternative to War and Surrender* (Illinois, 1962). Osgood suggested that it was possible to disarm unilaterally over a number of stages, giving the other side a chance to copy you at each stage. Here are some of the points he made.

1 Every step you take must be seen by your opponent as a real reduction in the threat to them, e.g. Britain should cancel Trident, not dispose of already obsolete weapons.
2 Every time you take a unilateral step, invite your opponent to do the same.
3 You should carry out unilateral acts whether or not your opponent promises to copy you.
4 Every time you carry out a new stage, give it full publicity in advance and full publicity after you have carried it out.
5 Concentrate on stages which your opponent is most likely to copy.
6 You should first carry out stages which involve the least risk to your safety.

## The Church and the Bomb

If you have been to London, you may have visited Westminster Abbey. Near the main entrance to the Abbey is a gateway leading to a large square with buildings on each side. In this square the atmosphere is usually peaceful and quiet, quite unlike the noise and bustle of the London streets outside. But one day in 1982 the peace surrounding Church House which is situated in the square, was shattered by the arrival of journalists, radio broadcasters and television cameras. The reason was that a committee set up two years previously was about to announce its conclusions about the attitude of the Church towards nuclear weapons. The book which contains this report was called *The Church and the Bomb*, and although it was the work of the Church of England alone, it remains one of the best-known statements of Christian opinion. By no means all Christians agree with it, and other books were written to oppose it, such as *The Cross and the Bomb*.

*The Church and the Bomb* asked two important questions: can a nuclear war ever be a just war? and is it wrong to possess nuclear weapons?

*Can a nuclear war ever be a just war?*

> We conclude that the conditions which a state must meet before it is ethically entitled to go to war could not be met by a nuclear power contemplating war against another nuclear power.
> (*The Church and the Bomb*)

> Any act of war which aims indiscriminately at the destruction of entire cities or wide areas with their inhabitants is a crime against God and man, to be firmly and unhesitatingly condemned.
> (The Papal Encyclical *Gaudium et Spes*)

Christians are fairly united in the view that a nuclear war can never be justified:
1 Vast numbers of unarmed civilians would die.

2 The evil inflicted by the war must be far greater than the degree of suffering which gave rise to the war.

3 War should be a last resort. There is a danger with nuclear weapons that since it is vital to strike first there may be a panic to be the first to attack before other means of sorting out the dispute have been thought through.

4 There should be a reasonable chance of success. How can there ever be victory in nuclear war?

Can you think of any other reasons why a nuclear war could not be a just war?

*Is it wrong to possess nuclear weapons?*

This is the question which divides most people, Christian and non-Christian alike.

*Arguments in favour of having nuclear weapons*

1 Nuclear weapons keep the peace. If both sides are equally powerful, neither will dare use them.

2 We have to persuade the enemy that we will use nuclear weapons to stop them from attacking us. We can only do this if we possess the weapons.

3 Possession of nuclear weapons has worked. There have been no major wars since 1945.

*Arguments against the possession of nuclear weapons*

1 'Even when armaments are not used, by their cost alone they kill the poor by causing them to starve.' (*The Holy See and Disarmament*)

2 If you do not have nuclear weapons on your soil you are far less likely to be the object of a nuclear attack. If the Russians do launch nuclear weapons it will be against countries which have nuclear weapons aimed at Russia.

3 If you threaten to annihilate your opponents you will cause them to panic. We are told that the Russians are aggressive by nature and would attack us given a chance. This is not so. In the Second World War Russia lost millions of people, and is determined that this will not happen again. They see the build-up of weapons in the West as a threat to them, and will only reduce their weapons if the West shows a genuine willingness to do so.

4 The more nuclear weapons there are in the world, the more likely nuclear war becomes. There are serious dangers that missiles may be launched by accident or fall into the hands of extremist groups who will not hesitate to use them.

---

### Statements for discussion

In any discussion of the complicated matter of nuclear weapons, it is difficult to know where to start. Here are some thoughts of the famous and the unknown alike. Use them as a starting point for your discussion.

## *On the possession of nuclear weapons*

As possessors of a vast nuclear arsenal, we must also be aware that not only is it wrong to attack civilian populations but it is wrong to threaten to attack them as part of a strategy of deterrence.

(*To Live in Christ Jesus*, US Catholic bishops)

The possession of tactical nuclear weapons makes smoother the path towards a general nuclear holocaust.

(James McCarthy, a Quaker)

Deterrence, which is the only alternative way of attempting to deal with human conflict, is based on the control of force by so directing its use that its worst effects are prevented.

(Graham Leonard, Bishop of London)

Only by maintaining a credible deterrent is it possible to make nuclear war less likely.

(Gerard Hughes)

## *On the use of nuclear weapons*

It is in this situation, where we might face obliteration as a people, that I would think it permissible to launch a nuclear response, if that response had any hope of preventing obliteration.

(Keith Ward)

Today, the scale and the horror of modern warfare, whether nuclear or not, makes it totally unacceptable as a means of settling differences between nations.

(Pope John Paul II)

## *On the cost of nuclear weapons*

Every gun that is made, every warship launched, every rocket fired, signifies in a final sense, a theft from those who hunger and are not fed, from those who are cold and not clothed.

(President Eisenhower)

Countries squander cash to boost their pride while millions starve. The money spent on arms is scandalous while schools, and homes and hospitals remain unbuilt.

(*Populorum Progressio*)

## *On the people behind them*

You can't really think about your future at this age, because who knows what's going to happen and we may not have a future if some kind of war breaks out.

I wouldn't like to survive because everything else would be gone and you would have nothing to look forward to.

Older people . . . have them, not us. We don't want them, so if it changed I think it will be someone from our generation. But it's going to take a little while.

(Thoughts of American teenagers)

A Japanese journalist, Mitsuko Shimomura, reported . . . that American and Russian educators undertook studies to investigate how their own country was introduced in the other's middle school textbooks. The Russian investigators found that the American textbooks presented the Soviet Union as a country that has a one-party dictatorship, that it is expansionist, that it is economically and politically behind the times, and lacks freedom.

A similarly unbalanced view was echoed in the report of the American team. They found that the Soviet textbooks portrayed America as a country plagued with unemployment, inflation, crime, social injustice and racial discrimination and exhibiting militaristic ambition.

(Nikkyo Niwano, a Buddhist writer)

. . . and when finally he (the American President) gets away to the golf course . . . at close hand, you may be sure, is that lonely, eerie and ever-present creature who stays never more than ten seconds from the president; the man who carries in his pocket the day's scrambler code that can flash the proper combination to the Red Box nuclear alert system of the Strategic Air Command in the bowels of the earth below Omaha, Nebraska.

(Alistair Cooke, *The Americans*)

## World faiths for peace

*The Church and the Bomb* came to the same sort of conclusions about the causes of violence as did the people at Corrymeela and Neve Shalom: it all boils down to distrust and fear. *The Church and the Bomb* makes the following suggestions as to how relationships between countries could be improved. Do you agree with any of these ideas? Have you any of your own?

1 Disarmament talks should be publicised and supported.

2 People should be educated so that they understand the real issues at stake between East and West. Everyone knows that the Russians are supposed to be our enemies. But how many of us know why?

3 We must try to understand other nations without making assumptions about them.

4 The Church is an international organisation and should use its opportunities to create peace projects. The Churches of East and West Germany have already made a start here.

5 We should strengthen cultural, sporting and academic ties between nations. These are all activities where people come together in peace to share matters that interest them.

6 The press should be careful not to spread hysteria by misrepresenting the so-called enemy in a totally aggressive attitude.

*. . . our duty is to the whole human family whom God took as his own, by sharing our life in Jesus. If we persist in pinning our hopes on nuclear weapons, we are simply gambling with the lives and the well-being of the innocent and the unborn. No considerations whatever can give us the right to do this. We believe that if we respond to this challenge, God will bless that response and use it to bring hope and healing to the world and to extend his kingdom of justice and peace.*

(The Church and the Bomb)

## Christians against the Bomb
### Christian CND

This is the specifically Christian branch of the CND. The organisation has the same aims as CND but the people who belong to it do so because they are Christian and they see their membership and activities as part of their Christian witness.

The logo shows a broken cross symbolising the death of man, and a circle representing the unborn child. The whole can be seen to represent the death of the unborn child. In the centre is the dove of peace. Members of Christian CND believe that the existence of nuclear weapons is contrary to the spirit of Christ, who taught his followers to be peacemakers. Christians worship a God who gives life to men, and they cannot support weapons which are made to wipe out whole populations, or policies which encourage us to think of people in other lands, whom we have never met, as enemies.

### Paxchristi

Paxchristi is the international Catholic Peace movement founded at the end of the Second World War. The aim of Paxchristi is 'to work with all for peace for all, witnessing always to the peace of Christ'. Members of Paxchristi are committed to prayer and non-violent living, and the organisation wants to make the teachings of the Church on the subject of peace better known. Like Amnesty International, Paxchristi is concerned also with prisoners of conscience, especially conscientious objectors who have been sent to prison for refusing to do military service. Paxchristi campaigns for nuclear disarmament and supports all efforts leading to multilateral disarmament, including the Campaign against the Arms Trade.

Paxchristi has many members who are not Catholic but who want to commit themselves to Christian principles.

### The Peace Tax Campaign

This campaign was founded by the Quakers. In these days many of us would not expect to fight in a war, but a vast proportion of our tax – an estimated 20% – is spent on weapons of war. The aim of the Peace Tax Campaign is to make the government agree that since conscientious objection is now allowed by many nations, it follows logically that a conscientious objector cannot be expected to pay for weapons: 'A man who hires a murderer most certainly shares the guilt of the murder.'

The aim is to set up a peacemaking fund. People who wish to do so can pay the proportion of their taxes which would have been spent on weapons into the Peace Fund which would then be used to set up peace projects.

---

**Something to discuss and write about**

1 Some people say that it is wrong for Christians to become involved in organisations like CND. What reasons do you think they have for saying this? Do you agree with them?

2 If some people are allowed to divert their 'arms tax' to a 'peace tax', is there a danger that other groups will also want to opt out of other parts of government spending? (For instance, some people who receive private medical treatment and pay for their children's education might say that they should not have to pay taxes towards the NHS and the Education budget.) Would this be a reasonable point of view?

3 Are you content that 20% of your taxes will be spent on arms? Are there other things you would rather see it spent on?

---

### The World Conference on Religion and Peace

> If the religions of the world get together to support Action for Justice and Peace, something that seems absurd may become possible.
>
> (Bishop Helder Camara)

Religion is a worldwide phenomenon, and apart from some extremists, most religious people want peace. Religious leaders have considerable authority in many countries, and are in a position to influence thousands of people. Ever since the beginning of the century there have been meetings between representatives of different religious opinions to see if the leaders of world faiths can sway their governments towards peace.

The World Conference for Religion and Peace was set up in Kyoto, Japan in 1970. As a worldwide organisation it has been able to pinpoint the most common causes of violence in the world, such as poverty, racism, oppression, the misuse of resources and the lack of human rights.

The WCRP has four main aims:

(a) To set in motion discussion between people of different religions and create a climate for the peaceful solution of disputes.

(b) To encourage the setting-up of national and regional interfaith groups for peace.

(c) To develop an interfaith presence in the United Nations.

(d) To encourage interfaith dialogue for peace.

[The role of religions is to] develop moral, ethical and religious influences wherever and whenever policy is made. It is to take political action and become effective in taking it. . . .

It is not enough for religion to mean well . . . but religion must DO well, act effectively.

(Dr Homer A. Jack)

People of religion . . . have a greater responsibility to the world and must minister to others. Everywhere in the world there are more people of faith than we think. Our task is . . . to awaken them.

(Bishop Helder Camara)

To encourage others to develop peace in their hearts, we must dismantle the armour around our own hearts. If one person distrusts others and is on their guard against them, these others will likewise adopt a defensive attitude. When we can face others with an open mind, they will relax and will open their hearts to us.

(Nikki Niwano, first chairman of the WCRP and a Buddhist)

## Punishment

Punishment on a national scale is carried out under the regulations of the law and is a form of violence to the individual. Offenders are hurt, and so are their families.

We have already seen that some people do commit acts of violence, and the problem has always been what to do about it. We also have to decide what action to take against the majority of offenders who do not commit violent crimes. From very early times, all societies developed some kind of legal system. This would normally include:

- *laws*: as it became clear that some members of communities did steal from and harm others, laws were made forbidding them to do so.
- *law enforcers*: judges were appointed to hear disputes. Later on, representatives of the community would arrest suspects rather then leave it to the individual to bring the accused to court.
- *punishments*: different ways were found of punishing offenders, often with a strong emphasis on making 'the punishment fit the crime'.

Like so many issues you are studying, the treatment of offenders is a very sensitive area. When a crime is committed, the victim and his or her friends may be in an emotional state, and they may say in no uncertain terms what they would like to do to the criminal if they could. This is perhaps a very good reason for *not* letting victims get their hands on those suspected of committing the crime, but for all suspects being dealt with by people not personally involved in the case, who can see the issues objectively. In this way, it is more likely that suspects will be treated as innocent unless or until they are proved guilty.

## Punishment in the Bible

You have already studied some passages in Matthew chapter 5. Look at these passages again and discuss how Jesus' teaching here might be applied to criminal offenders.

The Old Testament view was far less complex, and worked on a simple principle of paying back evil for evil. This principle is best seen in Exodus 21:23–5: 'Whatever hurt is done, you shall give life for life, eye for eye, tooth for tooth, hand for hand, foot for foot . . . .' Exodus 21 also mentions certain punishments for particular crimes. Make a list of the crimes and their punishments in two columns. Discuss whether you think the punishments are suitable. (See also Exodus 22:1–4.)

## Leave it to God?

Read the parable of the wheat and the tares (Matthew 13:24–30). This parable seems to suggest that it is God, the judge of all, who will actually sort out the wheat from the tares – or the 'good from the bad'. Many Jews, Christians and Muslims believe that after death we will be judged according to our deeds on earth, and Hinduism teaches that your next reincarnation will depend on the quality of your present life.

Does that mean that in the present life we can allow people to do what they want and get away with it because their deeds will catch up with them in a future life? Most people would say no, because of the distress caused to members of society by people who insist on hurting others. The ideal would be to prevent people from harming others, but if this is impossible, then do we have a responsibility to find a way of dealing with offenders after the event.?

## Motives

There are four different reasons commonly given for punishing offenders. Motives in punishing people are important, because on that depends the sort of punishment given. If you are a judge or a magistrate passing sentence on someone who has been found guilty of a crime, you have to ask yourself, 'What am I trying to achieve here?' One of the following would probably be your answer – or perhaps a combination of more than one.

**Revenge**: You may want to say on behalf of society, 'We want to get our own back. You did something unpleasant to this person, and now we want to give you a taste of your own medicine.'

**Deterrent**: Or you may say, 'I'm not out for revenge but I am going to stop you (deter you) or anyone else from doing that again. So I'm going to do something to you that'll make you, or anyone else who might consider doing what you did, think twice about it next time.'

**Reform**: Or you may say, 'My main concern is to stop you behaving in this way, and the only way to achieve that is to try to help you become the sort of person who does not *want* or *need* to commit crimes. I don't think that making your life unpleasant is going to make you feel any better disposed towards society so I'll try to find another way of making you a reformed character.'

**Protect society**: Or you may say, 'My main duty is to the community. I must do something which will mean that you are physically unable to be a nuisance to others for a long time.'

---

### Group work

Arrange yourselves into groups for next lesson. Before the lesson, everyone should find an account in the newspapers of a court case where the defendant has been found guilty. In your groups, select one or two cases and discuss what sentence you would give. Make sure that you decide what your motives are in passing sentence.

---

## Methods

There are a number of sentences commonly passed in British courts.

- prison, not only for crimes involving murder, violence, theft and sex attacks. The majority of people in British prisons are not there for any of these crimes.
- fines
- removal of driving licence
- community service
- meeting the victim and making up for what was done
- reparation.

For what sorts of crimes do you think these sentences would be suitable?

---

### Research

1 Find out about prison conditions in Britain today.
2 Find out about the work of societies who want prison reform such as the Howard League.
3 Try to arrange a visit from a prison chaplain and ask him or her to talk about his or her work.

### Extension work

1 Do you know anyone who has been the victim of a serious crime? Can the punishment of the offender make the victim feel better?
2 (a) If the offence is theft, should the value of the goods make any difference to the sentence?
  (b) If the crime was violent, should the sentence take into account the extent of the injuries?

---

*continued*

> 3 When passing sentence, should the court take into account the situation of the offender? Should the following be considered?
>    (a) past offences
>    (b) a psychiatric report
>    (c) home background
>    (d) state of health
>    (e) whether the offender has dependants who rely on his or her income.

Sometimes the fury of a whole nation is aroused by a particularly horrible crime. When a child murderer or rapist is on the loose, people's anger very quickly leads to talk of bringing back hanging. This is a way of expressing the deep angry emotions roused by the abuse or murder of an innocent person. But we need to control our emotions and examine capital punishment in a more detached and rational way.

## Capital punishment

'That one of you who is faultless shall throw the first stone.' Read John 7:53–8, 11. (It is usually printed at the end of John 21.) What light does this story throw on Jesus' attitude towards capital punishment?

On 12 July 1983 members of the House of Commons, and members of the General Synod of the Church of England both voted on a motion to bring back capital punishment. In both cases the motion was defeated – in the Synod by a massive 407–36 with 10 abstentions. Here are some of the arguments that were used in those debates. Discuss the arguments and add more of your own.

*Arguments in favour of capital punishment*
1 Revenge. A murderer has taken a life, and his life must be taken in return. As the Old Testament says, 'an eye for an eye, a tooth for a tooth'. The only suitable way of punishing someone for taking a life is to take his in return.
2 Killing the murderer is the only way that society can show its utter disapproval of the crime.
3 Capital punishment acts as a deterrent. People will think twice before killing if they know that they will hang if caught.
4 Society must be protected from murderers. The only guarantee that a killer will not kill again is to end his or her life.

*Arguments against capital punishment*
1 People who want capital punishment really only want revenge. This is a feeling unworthy of civilised men and women, and is not to be encouraged.
2 If you believe that killing is wrong, then capital punishment is wrong.

3 Killing the murderer will not bring back the victim.
4 Killing the murderer might give some satisfaction to the victim's family in the short term, but in the end it won't make them any happier.
5 It has not been established statistically that the death penalty does act as a deterrent. Even when there was hanging, between 1900 and 1949 only 1 in 12 of known murders ended with a hanging. So in fact a murderer had the odds in favour of not being hanged. Also, many murders are committed in the heat of the moment, and the murderer will not stop to ask what will happen if caught. Similarly well-planned premeditated murders do not take failure into account but work on the principle that the killer will not get caught. The idea that punishment acts as a deterrent is hard to prove. Prison sentences and confiscation of driving licences are thought to be deterrents, yet people still commit crimes, and drive dangerously.
6 Capital punishment inflicts more long-term suffering on the killer's relatives than on the killer.
7 There is always a chance that an innocent person will be hanged.
8 Capital punishment is degrading to society and also to the executioner.

## Some Christian points of view

The Methodist Church welcomed the abolition by Parliament of Capital Punishment and is opposed to its reintroduction.

If justice is not done and seen to be done, people will start taking the law into their own hands.

The degrading effect of Capital Punishment on all concerned, prison staff, governors, judges and in the end all who support such a system is nothing less than a violation of the image of God in each one of us.

# Epilogue: What about the future?

This has not been an easy book to write, and it has probably not been very easy to study in places. It has introduced you to only a few of the very serious problems which face all thinking people today. Hopefully you will have realised that this is only a beginning, and that there is much to find out about all the topics introduced in this book.

One question which all the topics raise must be, 'Where do we go from here?' We all have a choice. Once we are made aware of the injustices, cruelties and unfairness which exists in this world – alongside a fair quantity of beauty, justice and kindness – we can do one of two things. We can go home, shut the door and pretend that none of these things are really happening, or that if they do, they have nothing to do with us. If everyone did this, the few people who have the power to cause misery will be in an even stronger position. Or of course, we can decide that we will try to change the things that cause misery and injustice.

Many people say that they want the world to be a better place for their children. What do they mean by this? Some parents, feeling that as children they went without many material goods, lavish expensive presents on their children, take them on expensive holidays, give them a lot of pocket money. Is this what is meant by making the world a better place for them?

Other people take a very different view. They say that they do not want their children to live under the shadow of the threat of nuclear war. They do not want their children to live in a world where large numbers of people, who are in some way oppressed, usually by the rich and powerful, feel that they have to resort to violence if the people who have the power to change things are to listen to them. Such people might feel that it is not good for children to grow up in a world where the constant striving for more money and more possessions is the main goal of life. They may not want their children to grow up caring little for the rights of the other creatures with whom we share this planet. They may want to halt the search for constant progress which results in poisonous fumes being released into the atmosphere and atomic waste into the sea.

**Some final thoughts for discussion**

1 What six things would you most like to see changed for the better before your children are born? What do you think people like yourself might do to bring about these changes?

2 Why is it important that we do think about the needs of future generations?

3 In what ways do you think Church leaders and leaders of other religions might help to make the world a better place for everyone?

'God, give us the grace to accept with serenity the things that cannot be changed, courage to change the things that should be changed, and the wisdom to distinguish the one from the other.'

(Reinhold Niebuhr)

# Course work

It is likely that you will be asked to present a number of pieces of course work on this part of the syllabus for GCSE. Your teacher will probably have explained to you the *Assessment Objectives*. It is very important that you understand what they are. They can be sum-marised as follows:

You will be expected to show three skills in each piece of your work. These skills are generally described as:

(a) factual knowledge/recall
(b) understanding
(c) evaluation.

In simple terms factual knowledge or recall means stating the facts, or 'telling the story' without any comment. In a piece of work marked out of 20, you might only be able to get a maximum of 8 marks for factual knowledge. This means that you must be careful not to devote too much of your work just to narrating the facts.

'Understanding' can cover many things and might also take up about 8 marks out of a possible 20. It might mean having to explain how religious texts can be applied in our society, e.g. 'What does the New Testament teach about the use of money?' is a factual question, but 'How can a Christian today put this teaching into practice in his or her life?' requires understanding. You might be asked to compare or contrast two different ideas, or show that you understand the full meaning of a text or a belief. Regarding the sort of subject matter covered in this book you will often be asked to show that you understand the arguments for and against a certain statement or standpoint. You might also be asked to select material from a religious tradition to illustrate a point, e.g. 'Give an account of, and explain the meaning of two stories from the New Testament which suggest a basis for Christian behaviour towards people of other races.' Many exam candidates find this very difficult to do, so beware!

'Evaluation' usually means giving your own point of view and stating your reasons for why you have reached this opinion. It may involve you having to argue 'how far' or 'to what extent' a certain belief is relevant today; or it may require you to put yourself into another person's shoes and say how you would feel if you were in their position. Evaluation accounts for the further 4 out of the 20 marks.

**Further suggestions for course work**

The following are suggestions for course work. They are only topics, and to ensure that you fulfill assessment objectives (a), (b) and (c) it is important that you, with the help of your teacher, make a structured question (like those in the following Table) out of the suggested topic.

1 The authority of sacred texts as a basis for moral behaviour in two or three religions.
2 Beliefs about creation and conservation in two or three religions.
3 A project to assist the unemployed run by a religious group.
4 Attitudes towards money in two or three religious traditions.
5 A project run by a religious organisation to aid the Third World.
6 A comparison of attitudes towards poverty within one religious tradition.
7 Attitudes towards poverty in two or three religions – a comparison.
8 A study of liberation theology: its main exponents, aims and achievements.
9 Religion and politics – a study of one religion, or a study of two or three.
10 A special study of an individual concerned with religion and politics.
11 Attitudes to race in one or more religions.
12 A special study of a person representing a religious tradition who has worked in the area of race relations.
13 Interfaith dialogue. What it is – illustrated with at least one example.
14 The work of the Council of Christians and Jews.
15 The work of the Runnymede Trust, or another organisation working for race relations.
16 The work of the World Council for Religion and Peace.
17 An account of a discussion on any issue studied with a fellow pupil of a religion different from your own. (Some boards may allow you to present a tape of such a discussion.)
18 Marriage and its meaning in one or more religions (or in two different Christian traditions).
19 A report on a visit to any relevant place of interest related to the course, e.g a hospice.
20 A study of feminist theology.
21 The place of women in religious traditions.
22 The debate over the ordination of women.
23 Religion and family structures including male/female roles and the upbringing of children.
24 An analysis of a TV programme on any relevant subject (there are many programmes on Sundays which could be of particular interest here).
25 Medical ethics. (There are many possibilities here.)

26 The work of a hospice.
27 War in religious traditions.
28 The just war theory.
29 Religious attitudes to the possession of nuclear weapons.
30 The work of Christian CND.
31 The work of Pax Christi.
32 Attiudes towards punishment in religious traditions.
33 A review of a relevant book you have read, e.g. *Bias to the Poor*, one of Desmond Tutu's books, *The Church and the Bomb*.

This list is only a beginning. Look out particularly for anything happening in your community which would serve as a relevant topic, such as the Truro project with the unemployed mentioned earlier. You will enjoy your work more as a rule if you can actually interview people and see for yourself what is going on rather than just reading about it in books. You will not be able to write about first hand experiences for all your pieces of course work, but do try to use this technique for at least one.

The following examples are based on a piece of work carrying 20 marks which are divided as follows:
K8
U8
E4

Check the weighting for the course you are taking very carefully. It will probably not be the same. However, you should be able to use the ideas given as examples of K, U, and E work whatever the weighting may be for your Examination Board.

ANALYSIS OF C/W TOPICS (Examples only, showing approximate allocation of marks out of a possible total of 20.)

| Topic | Factual recall (approx. 8 marks) | Understanding (approx. 8 marks) | Evaluation (approx. 4 marks) |
|---|---|---|---|
| **Laws and rules in religious traditions** | An account of the important rules or code of behaviour in the religion or religions you have chosen. | Either: an analysis of the meaning of relevant texts. Or: an explanation of how these rules have influenced relevant societies. | Discuss how possible it is to apply such rules in today's society. Or: discussion as to how far personal behaviour can depend solely on rules. What other guidelines should be used in forming a personal standard of behaviour? |
| **Creation and conservation** | A description of the creation stories in two different religious traditions. | How the ideas contained in these stories have influenced attitudes towards the created order. | An evaluation of the creation myths chosen. Do they have any value for today? Or: an evaluation of the work of one conservation society. |
| **A project run by a religious group to help the unemployed** | A description of the project. | Explanation of why the project is necessary. What religious principles lie behind the project? Why should a 'religious' group want to help the unemployed? | Evaluate the effectiveness of the project. How would you develop it? Do you think that this sort of activity has a place in the life of a religious community? |
| **An interview with a woman who feels that she is called to be a priest** | An account of the interview giving the arguments put forward by the woman. | Show that you understand the arguments of those who say that women should not be ordained to the priesthood. | Put yourself in the woman's position. How would you feel? Give your own view on this subject. |
| **A weekend spent in a monastery/ convent** | An account of the work of the community. Include details of the 'rule'. | Show that you understand the principles on which people have chosen to live a monastic life. How far are these principles based on religious texts? | Do you think that members of 'religious' communities make a contribution to society? How would you feel about spending your whole life in such an order? |

# Bibliography

Afza and Ahmead, *The Position of Women in Islam* (1982)
Ahmead, *Islam, its Meaning and Message* (Islamic Foundation, 1975)
Baelz, *Ethics and Belief* (1977)
Barclay, *The Plain Man's Guide to Ethics* (Fount, 1973)
Barnett, *A Jewish Family in Britain* (RMEP)
Bartley, *Morality and Religion* (Macmillan, 1971)
Bennett, *Christian Social Ethics in a Changing World* (SCM, 1966)
Birnie, *Focus on Christianity* (Arnold, 1969–78)
Bowker, *Problems of Suffering in the Religions of the World* (CUP, 1979)
Brown, *Choices – Ethics and the Christian* (Blackwell, 1983)
Butler, *Life Among the Hindus* (Arnold, 1980)
Carmody (ed.), *Women in World Religions* (Abingdon, 1979)
Catholic Social Welfare Commission, various publications
Cheston, *It's Your Life* (RMEP, 1984)
Chignall, *Perspectives* (Arnold, 1981)
The Christian Ecology Group, *God's Green World* (1983)
Church Information Office, *The Church and the Bomb*
——, various other publications
Cole, *A Sikh Family in Britain* (RMEP, 1985)
Community and Race Relations Unit of the British Council of Churches,
    various publications
Cragg, *Islam and the Muslim* (OUP, 1978)
Cupitt, *The Crisis of Moral Authority* (Lutterworth)
Elliott and Pain, *Sex, Marriage and Family Life* (Lutterworth, 1975)
Erricker, *Christian Ethics* (Lutterworth, 1984)
Ewan and Pancholi, *Hindu Home* (CEM, in press)
Field, *Christianity in the Modern World* (Hulton, 1983)
Field and Toon, *Real Questions* (Lion, 1983)
Fletcher, *The One and Only Me* (Denholm, 1975)
Fletcher, *Situation Ethics* (SCM)
Friends Home Services Committee, various publications
Gorman, *The Society of Friends* (RMEP, 1978)
Gower, *Frontiers* (Lion, 1982)
Greenpeace, various publications
Haring, *Medical Ethics*
Harrison and Shepherd, *A Christian Family in Britain* (RMEP, 1985)
——, *A Muslim Family in Britain* (RMEP)
Hemming, *Individual Morality* (Panther, 1970)
Hill and Mathews (eds), *Race – A Christian Symposium* (Gollancz, 1968)
Holland, *Duties of the Brotherhood in Islam* (Islamic Foundation, 1975)
Honderich, *Punishment, the Supposed Justification* (Pelican, 1971)
Huddleston, *Naught for your Comfort* (Fount, 1977)
Irving, *Islam and Social Responsibility* (Islamic Foundation, 1974)
Jacobs, *The Book of Jewish Belief* (Behrman, 1984)
Jayatilleke, *Aspects of Buddhist Social Philosophy* (Buddhist Publication Society)
Jewish Educational Bureau, various publications
Kamel, *Islam and the Race Question* (UNESCO, 1970)
Keeling, *Morals in a Free Society* (SCM, 1970)

Mackinnon (ed.), *Making Moral Decisions* (SPCK)
Mawdudi, *Birth Control* (Islamic Publications, 1968)
——, *The Ethical View Point of Islam* (Islamic Publications)
Methodist Church Division of Social Responsibility, various publications
Millard (ed.), *Religion and Medicine* (SCM)
Montenant, Plateaux and Roux, *How to Read the World* (SCM, 1985)
Moss (ed.), *God's Yes to Sexuality* (Fount, 1981)
Mullen, *Beginning Philosophy* (Arnold, 1984)
——, *Thinking about Religion* (Arnold, 1984)
——, *Working with Morality* (Arnold, 1983)
New Internationalist, *The Peace Pack*
Nowell-Smith, *Ethics* (Pelican, 1954)
Palmer and Bisset, *Worlds of Difference* (Blackie, 1985)
Prickett, *Marriage and the Family* (Lutterworth, 1985)
Prickett (ed.), *Death* (Lutterworth, 1980)
Pringle, *Christianity in Action Today* (Schofield and Simms, 1968)
Radhakrishnan, *The Hindu View of Life* (1927)
Ray and Bridger, *A Hindu Family in Britain* (RMEP, 1985)
Richardson, *The Biblical Doctrine of Work* (SCM, 1963)
RMEP, Charities Series
St John, *Religion and Social Justice* (RMEP, 1985)
Sangharakshita, *Buddhism, World Peace and Nuclear War* (Windhorse, 1984)
Sarwarg, *Islam Beliefs and Teachings* (Muslim Educational Trust)
Schumacher, *Small is Beautiful* (Abacus, 1973)
SCM/CEM, Probe Series
Sheppard, *Bias to the Poor* (Hodder, 1984)
Sider, *Rich Christians in an Age of Hunger* (Hodder, 1971)
Sidhu, *A Brief Introduction to Sikhism* (Sikh Missionary Society, 1973)
——, *The Sikh Woman* (Sikh Missionary Society)
Smedes, *Mere Morality* (Lion, 1983)
Story, *Buddhist Lay Ethics* (Buddhist Publications)
Taylor, *Focus on Faith* (Murray, 1985)
——, *Focus on Life* (Murray, 1981)
Taylor, *Enough is Enough* (SCM, 1975)
Taylor and Lipman, *Judaism – Peace and Disarmament* (Leeds Jonah)
Trudgian, *Who is my Neighbour?* (Denholm, 1975)
Ward, *Ethics and Christianity* (1970)
Ward and Dubois, *Only one Earth* (Penguin)
Wigoder, *Jewish Values* (Keter, 1974)
Wogman, *On Dying Well* (Church Information Office)
——, *Abortion* (Church Information Office)
——, *Decisions about Life and Death* (Church Information Office)

# Index